STEVE MIZERAK'S
COMPLETE BOOK OF
POOL

STEVE MIZERAK with MICHAEL E. PANOZZO

CB
CONTEMPORARY BOOKS

Library of Congress Cataloging-in-Publication Data

Mizerak, Steve, 1944–
    Steve Mizerak's complete book of pool / Steve Mizerak with
Michael E. Panozzo.
        p.   cm.
    Includes index.
    ISBN 0-8092-4255-9
    1. Pool (Game).   I. Panozzo, Michael E.   II. Title.
GV891.M686   1990
794.7'3—dc20   90-39589
                                            CIP

Cover design by Georgene Sainati
Cover photograph by Carmine R. Manicone Photography

Published by Contemporary Books
A division of NTC/Contemporary Publishing Group, Inc.
4255 West Touhy Avenue, Lincolnwood (Chicago), Illinois 60712-1975 U.S.A.
Printed in the United States of America
International Standard Book Number: 0-8092-4255-9

  19 20 21 22 23 24 25 26 27 28 29 30 CUS/CUS 0 1 9 8 7 6 5 4 3

To Richard Black, for renewing my interest in pool

To the K mart Corporation, for showing a keen interest
in a sport most corporations forget

Contents

Foreword

It's certainly no secret that pool is enjoying a resurgence in popularity these days. Plush new poolrooms abound, the game is receiving a great deal of exposure in both print and electronic media, and millions of people of all ages are flocking to the pool table for enjoyment and competition.

It's great to see pool attracting all of these new players. I think it's a pity it has taken so long for so many people to realize the beauty and challenge pool offers.

I consider myself very fortunate to have been around pool almost all my life. It's difficult to say that I was initially drawn to the game by pool's beauty. At four years old, you don't see a lot of innate beauty in things. That's how old I was when my father, Steve, Sr., introduced me to the magic wand and 15 colored balls. I was fascinated by the colors and intrigued by the sight of the balls rolling around the table and into pockets.

I was born in Perth Amboy, New Jersey. Being an only child, I spent a great deal of time with my father. Aside from working in a wireworks factory, my father also happened to be one of the best pool players in Jersey. He won the New Jersey state pocket billiards championship several times.

My father was also a tremendous baseball player. He played some AA and AAA baseball but ended up playing professionally in Canada in the Outlaw League. The Outlaw League was made up mostly of American players who had run into problems in the U.S. leagues. My father's "problem" stemmed from an umpire-bashing incident that occurred while he was in the minor leagues. Nonetheless, he was a terrific second baseman and was player/manager of several teams.

(courtesy of Carmine R. Manicone Photography)

When in Perth Amboy, however, Dad was down at Madison Recreation every day, and I always tagged along. Madison Rec was a great room in the old tradition—25 or so tables, designed for serious pool playing. And the room attracted *serious* pool players. As a youth I was treated to unforgettable appearances by legends like Willie Mosconi, Irving

Here I practice under the watchful eye of the late Onofrio Lauri, a terrific player from New York. I was still in college at the time of this photo, and Lauri was a great friend. He taught me a lot about demeanor at the table and composure while playing. He also taught me how to carry myself away from the table. Lauri was a true gentleman.

Crane, and, yes, even His Heaviness—Rudolph "Minnesota Fats" Wanderone. I'll never forget the day Fats played my father and *literally* fell through the floor. They were playing a match and old Fatty hit a loose plank in the floor, and *Wham!* Fats went knee-deep into the ground.

Surrounded with characters and atmosphere like that, it's little wonder that the game grabbed me into its clutches. But while curiosity initially drew me to pool, what kept me coming back was the fact that I was very good right from the start. You've seen children on TV who are concert pianists and violinists. Child prodigies, they're often called. Well, I was a pool prodigy.

My father saw my ability and installed a pool table in a shed in our backyard. He built up a floor around the table that allowed me to reach most shots. For shots out in the middle of the table, I dragged around an old Coke box to stand on. Dear old Dad even bought Madison Rec from the owner, Jim Croger, when I was eight years old.

Despite my natural ability at pocket billiards, my father's true desire was for me to become a professional baseball player. I don't know if he foresaw the astronomical salaries ballplayers would be earning, but he did know about pool—and in that game, there simply wasn't much money to be made. Dad even went so far as to transform me from a right-handed child to a left-handed one. Good left-handed baseball pitchers were at a premium, he figured. Always playing the percentages.

I gave baseball a try but gave up on it in high school. I came in to pitch one game and, while I threw the ball with pretty good velocity, accuracy was not one of my strong suits. I walked four straight hitters and never threw a strike. My coach took me out and stuck me in right field, a spot normally reserved for the worst player on the team.

After that, I concentrated on pool. I still did other things. I played basketball a lot. It was my second favorite sport . . . until I discovered golf. Then I gave up basketball, and golf became my second love. But I *always* had time for pool. I can honestly say there

(courtesy of *Billiards Digest*)

Winning the 1982 PPPA World Open was very important to me. It proved I was far from "over the hill," as some players had suggested.

was never a time in my life when I wanted to give up on it. Pool was the constant in my life.

Maybe it was the continual challenge pool offered that made me stick with the game. There is always room for improvement . . . working toward the perfect game or the perfect match. That challenge kept me going during the early years, when I started playing and winning local and state championships. It aided me when I saw players like Luther Lassiter and "Cowboy" Jimmy Moore lift the game to seemingly unthinkable heights during matches at Madison Rec. And it gave me a boost during difficult periods of my life, like the late seventies, when things were not so great in my career and other players insisted that I was washed up. I accepted the challenge and proved everyone wrong by winning back-to-back world championships in 1982 and 1983.

The challenge pool offers will drive you, too, as you become more fanatical about the game. You'll realize early on that excelling at pool takes more than just talent. You have to

be a student of the game. I learned a great deal from several different people. My father instilled the drive and pride. An old-timer named E. J. "Doc" Hazzard taught me a lot about safety play.

As much as anything, however, I learned from *watching*. I studied great players—what they did, when they did it, why they did what they did, and how they did it. Once I understood their reasoning, I tried to emulate them. You had to be a great watcher back then, because in those days the great players didn't share their secrets.

One suggestion before we delve deeper into the game: don't try to do or learn too much too quickly. You can't develop flawless technique and knowledge overnight. I played

ix

for nearly 10 years before I really understood position play. Then again, I started when I was four years old, so it took a while for the knowledge to sink in! Still, my father always told me, "Patience. It will come." Well, he was right. It seemed like all of a sudden everything made sense. All of that information and the ideas I had stored in my head started making sense. It's a wonderful feeling when it all comes together.

One of the things that intrigued me about pool when I was young was that I was able to beat men who were 30 and 40 years old. I found that really interesting. When I was 15, I was already one of the best players in New Jersey. A kid beating grown-ups—that, to me, was intriguing.

Today, the intrigue is strictly desire-driven. I've been doing this all my life, and I still look for ways to improve. I still feel like I can win any tournament I enter. I can still compete.

And, again, there's the challenge of mastering the game. To me, there's no greater sense of accomplishment than that which comes from conquering the mysteries of pocket billiards.

It won't take you very long to agree.

Acknowledgments

Very special thanks go to The Billiard Archive in Pittsburgh and to *Billiards Digest* in Chicago. To Mr. Mike Shamos of the former, heartfelt thanks for allowing access to the incredible wealth of information you've worked so tirelessly to accumulate (and somehow catalogue!). To Mr. Mort Luby, Jr., of the latter, many thanks for permission to sift through *Billiards Digest*'s extensive photo file. If not for the unique photos and illustrations from both The Billiard Archive and *Billiards Digest*, the book would have been much thinner and a tad less interesting!

Special thanks also go to Joe Newell for the intriguing patents information and diagrams he was willing to share, and to William Hendricks, whose *History of Billiards* provided invaluable information on a host of topics covered herein. Thanks also to Billie Billing for photos of the modern-day players.

To Bear Lakes Country Club in West Palm Beach, Florida, thanks for making the World of Leisure "Trafalgar" table available for the instructional photos. Special credit goes to Carmine Manicone for his terrific photography on the instructional portion of the book and for the beautiful cover photo, taken at Gil Stienman's new poolroom, Celebrity Billiards, in West Palm Beach.

Today's poolroom is long on elegance and sophistication, and short on barroom brawls.

1
The Billiard-Room Boom

America is currently experiencing what I call a "Poolroom Boom." Plush new billiard gathering places now occupy some of the hottest locales in the country's largest, most cosmopolitan cities. While this latest trend is changing the setting of the game from the stark, dank rooms of yesteryear, it's not the first time billiards has undergone such a dramatic surge in popularity.

Perhaps the longest continuous run of success enjoyed by billiard rooms and the game's finest players was in the 1920s and 1930s. Spurred on by enormous popularity at the turn of the century, interest in billiards—both the pocket and carom disciplines—reached an all-time high in the twenties. It is estimated that more than 40,000 billiard rooms were open during the 20-year period between 1922-1941. New York City alone was said to have a staggering 4,000 billiard rooms!

Not even the Great Depression could slow the industry's charge. The rooms of those days were monstrous shrines that drew players from all levels of the social strata. Captains of industry and politicians shared quarters with blue-collars and hustlers.

The trademark of billiard rooms during the boom was size—20-table rooms were considered rather small in those days. The major New York billiard arenas included the famed Hoppe-Peterson Club, a 42-table room co-owned by world Straight-Rail champion Willie Hoppe, and, later, Julian Billiard Academy. (Straight-Rail is a form of carom billiards which was popular in the United States until the thirties.) Julian's, a 30-plus table room opened by Frank Julian in 1933, has miraculously endured the incredible swings in the popularity of the game and still calls 14th Street on the city's Lower East Side home. Philadelphia, which later spawned a handful of the game's greatest players, boasted the 40-table Allinger's and the 70-table Hudson Recreation.

Chicago, the "City of Broad Shoulders," surely needed a strong back to support the weight of Bensinger's and Mussy's. Louis Bensinger's recreation facility featured nearly 90 tables on two floors (one for pool, the other for billiards) in the heart of the city's downtown area. White-gloved rack men handled the grooming and preparation of the tables, while waitresses checked coats and took drink orders. Elegant paintings adorned the walls between velvet-curtained windows.

Not even Bensinger's, though, which lasted until the late seventies, could come

This entire seven-story building housed little besides billiards and bowling. "The Recreation," Detroit's mammoth health spa, featured 103 billiard tables and nearly 100 bowling alleys in its 125,000-square-foot encasement.

close to the colossal size of Detroit Recreation. A seven-story corner building with 125,000 square feet of space, "The Rec" boasted 103 tables in 1920. Besides 12 English Billiards tables, 53 carom tables, and 38 pocket billiard tables, the Rec had 88 bowling lanes. Irv Huston's billiard mecca also advertised 20 barber chairs, three manicuring stands, 14 cigar stands, a lunch counter on each floor, four soda fountains, a restaurant that could seat 300, and a special exhibition room with theater seating for 250 spectators!

It's no coincidence that the era also produced two of the greatest cue men of all time—Willie Hoppe and Ralph Greenleaf. Greenleaf, who won the first of his 14 world titles in 1919, was an extraordinary talent. A native of tiny Monmouth, Illinois, the tall, handsome Greenleaf was a born showman. He brought flash and charm to the pocket game—which had, to that point, been looked on as a cheap stepchild of the more sophisticated Straight-Rail and Balkline disciplines. Married to a vaudeville actress, Princess Nai-Tai-Tai, Greenleaf parlayed his skills as a cue marksman and his natural flair for the stage into a lucrative career that spanned nearly 30 years.

Greenleaf, Hoppe, and other stars of the day (Charles Peterson, Welker Cochran, Frank Taberski, Jake Schaefer, Jr., and more) were accorded sports celebrity status. Several were featured in national advertising campaigns for various companies, and many were pictured on the cigarette cards which were so popular at the time.

There are numerous parallels between the billiard-room boom of the twenties and thirties and the current poolroom heyday. For one, the most successful and fashionable rooms were in the heart of America's largest cities. During the sixties and seventies, when urban decay led to suburban flight, rooms left with the patrons.

Today, the folks who fled to the suburbs have made a U-turn. Young professionals, who doubtlessly played the game in family rec rooms throughout the 'burbs, are back in the city, and pool brings nostalgia for an age that refuses to grow old.

But it's not just the game that attracts people to billiard rooms. In his 1967 book called *Hustlers, Beats and Others*, sociologist Ned Polsky contended that the poolroom satisfied "an essential social function." In reviewing the success of poolrooms in the twenties and thirties, Polsky further surmised that the rooms offered men a much needed sanctuary from women. Gradual acceptance of women in the poolroom, Polsky summarized, spelled doom for this "all-male institution."

Like the highly successful rooms of the twenties and thirties, the poolroom of the nineties (which actually started to take root around 1987) has made great strides in serving a broader social function. Today's boom, however, is also due in no small part to droves of women who are chalking up. A casual, relaxed social setting without the gamesmanship and intimidation of singles' hangouts is one of the main draws the "new" poolrooms have for young urban dwellers. "A modern approach to an old-fashioned lifestyle," said one New Yorker.

(courtesy of The Billiard Archive)

Billiards was strictly a man's game at the turn of the twentieth century.

Billiard rooms with 40 or more tables were
hardly uncommon in the 1920s.

"C. C. C." Carom and Pocket Billiard Parlors, 1511 Harney Street, Omaha, Neb.

Anyone who has played pool in taverns knows that a game now costs from fifty cents to two bucks. Ever wonder what the first coin-operated tables set a player back?

The first "automatic billiard table" was patented in 1903 by the Automatic Billiard Table Company. The rationale behind the invention was to dispense with the services of an attendant in public saloons. Balls were stored in a drawer beneath the table, and the insertion of a coin was required to release them. The balls could only be removed after the mechanism was again locked. As with today's coin-op tables, a pocketed ball returned along wooden troughs underneath the slate, into the drawer.

The cost of a game on the first pay-for-play table? One penny.

(courtesy of The Billiard Archive)

The first coin-operated billiard table cost all of a penny a game in 1903.

That modern approach comes in a variety of forms. A good many rooms opened since 1988 target the young, professional, after-work crowd. Gentlemen in jackets and ties, ladies in business suits, and leather briefcases abound, and cappuccino, pastries, and pasta salads have replaced beer and peanuts as standard fare. The settings are plush. Barley's Billiards in Atlanta and Mr. Lucky's and Muddler's in Chicago are three such rooms. Jillian's, with locations in Boston and Miami, also fits the mold.

Q's, with its fashionable Wilshire Boulevard address in Los Angeles, all but breaks the mold. Valet parking is offered, but only if patrons measure up to a very strict dress code. "I've told people to go home and get dressed," says Q's owner, Yossi Kviatkovsky, who custom built the 11 tables housed on two levels. "They come back an hour later dressed to the hilt!"

What makes Beverly Hills residents wait hours for a table? "This is the 'Hard Rock Cafe' with something to do," muses Kviatkovsky.

While poolrooms like Q's and Mr. Lucky's may draw the "shirts and ties," rooms like The Billiard Club in New York and Society Billiards in Miami attract a different crowd altogether. The motif in these halls is more "billiard bordello" than swank, and there is no sparing the volume on monster stereo systems.

Still another option in new billiard

(photo by Jay Good)

Champagne and Eight-Ball have combined to make rooms like Jillian's in Kendall, Florida, haute spots.

(photo by Sandra Tatum)

Q's in Los Angeles features tables custom-made by one of the room's owners, as well as valet parking!

(photo by Ron Gordon)

While some of today's new rooms are heavy on brass and mahogany, rooms like Muddler's Poolroom in Chicago take a more understated tack in decor.

(courtesy of The Billiard Club)

Yet another approach in modern poolroom decor is what can be called "billiard bordello," a look that has made The Billiard Club one of the hottest rooms in Manhattan.

rooms is the "player's" room. Designed in the tradition of the old school of pool halls, New York's Chelsea Billiards, Florida's Boca Billiards, and Obelisk of Newport News, Virginia, fit such a description. Clean and airy, the focus of these rooms is on lighting, quality equipment, and at least semi-serious play.

Regardless of a person's sex or personal style, most major metropolitan areas now feature a room that will satisfy everyone's needs. If not today, possibly tomorrow. It's been estimated that a new poolroom is opening somewhere around the country every day!

⚜ TOP 10 ROOMS ⚜

A listing of the top 10 new rooms (opened between January 1987 and August 1989) in the United States, as rated by *Billiards Digest* magazine of Chicago.

1. Barley's Billiards, Marietta, Georgia
2. Chelsea Billiards, New York City
3. Jillian's, Boston
4. Society Billiards, Miami
5. Golden Eight Ball Billiards, Phoenix
6. Anchorage Billiard Palace, Anchorage, Alaska
7. Muddler's Poolroom, Chicago
8. The Charlie Horse, North Abington, Massachusetts
9. Obelisk Billiard Club, Newport News, Virginia
10. Boca Billiards, Boca Raton, Florida

⚜ THE FEMALE PERSUASION ⚜

Women are taking up pool in ever-growing numbers. In fact, a 1987 survey of pool participation estimated that women now make up one third of the total pool-playing population. That translates to more than 10 million women players! Further, the survey found that nearly *half* of the 4.5 million Americans classified as "new participants" were women.

What more and more women are discovering is that playing pool involves no inherent physiological barriers. Men have no built-in advantage over women, just as a 26-year-old has no built-in advantage over a 50-year-old and a six-foot, 250-pounder has no edge against a five-foot, 120-pounder.

The quality of play among women at the professional level gets better and better each year. Experience—years and years of playing at home and on the road—is about all that separates men and women at the highest levels.

When I was growing up, I heard of a great woman player named Ruth McGinnis. I never saw her play, but her achievements were impressive. While there were virtually no tournaments, and her status as "world champion" was kept intact more from lack of competition than any other reason, she must have been good. Any person who could run 100 balls on the old narrow-pocket 5-by-10-foot tables—which McGinnis was said to have done—had to be great.

I did see Dorothy Wise play in her prime. She was a terrific player, having won five consecutive BCA U.S. Open titles—as a grandmother! She was a charming lady and a great competitor.

Ruth McGinnis, a child billiard prodigy, went on to become one of the sport's most revered women players. Without any tournaments in which to compete, however, her true skills were never really put to the test.

Possibly the second-best woman player ever was a little-known Japanese star named Mieko Harada. She played in the United States several times and won the 1974 World Invitational in Los Angeles. There wasn't much competition for her in Japan, and she only played here a few times, but I could tell from watching her that she was in a special class of players.

For my money, though, the greatest woman player of all time is Jean Balukas. I don't care how good McGinnis is said to have been. You simply can't compare long runs in exhibition play to the pressure of tournament play.

Jean Balukas is a great tournament player. She won the first of her seven BCA U.S. Open titles in 1972—when she was 12 years old! She also won six World Open 14.1 crowns and the 1988 World Open Nine-Ball title. On top of that, she owns a still-unbroken string of 16 consecutive Women's Professional Billiards Association Nine-Ball titles. Balukas has even competed in a handful of men's pro events, with moderate success.

While Balukas's talent is extraordinary, women should remember that the game is no different for them than it is for men. Women can learn the game the same way men do. Strength is not a huge factor in pool. In fact, a delicate touch—a trait most women seem to have—is probably more important than strength.

Practice and knowledge of what you're doing (*i.e.*, experience) are all that's needed to excel. Good hand-eye coordination is also recommended.

(courtesy of *Billiards Digest*)

(courtesy of *Billiards Digest*)

Dorothy Wise, a classy California grandmother, won five straight Billiard Congress of America U.S. Open titles, from 1967 to 1971.

Japan's Mieko Harada has all the skills necessary to dominate the game for a long time. Lack of competition in her homeland may have kept her from reaching her true potential.

(courtesy of Corley Associates)

Jean Balukas is, without a doubt, the greatest woman pocket billiard player of all time. She's so good, in fact, that she's even entered a handful of men's tournaments in recent years—a move that she and I have discussed at great length!

(courtesy of The Billiard Archive)

PLANES, TRAINS, AND AUTOMOBILES

Some people love billiards so much they simply have to play when they're on the road. I don't mean just when they're out of town—I'm talking about playing on or in moving vehicles! If you think it's tough enough to sink a ball on a level table under perfect conditions, imagine what it would be like if you and the equipment were pitching, rolling, sliding, hopping, braking, and diving. Here's a look at ways of playing billiards while on the move.

SHIPS

Probably the earliest effort to provide billiards to travelers was on ocean liners. Voyages were long, and passengers yearned for recreation. Ships also tended to be outfitted in a grand style that might befit a fancy club and had all the appropriate amusements. The *Great Eastern*, a British vessel in regular service in the North Atlantic in the 1860s, boasted a billiard table, but no attempt was made to steady the table against the swaying of the sea, and playing conditions were, reportedly, highly unfavorable. The battle cruiser *HMS Renown*, of

World War I vintage, had a table in the officers' mess. Let's face it, though—you just can't play on a rolling ship. Unless the ocean is as calm as a lake or the boat is at anchor, there's no hope. This problem gave rise to some ingenious proposals.

If you can't keep the table still, a different solution is to make sure the balls won't move when the ship lists. It's tough to do this with round balls, so a game was developed for cruise ships using flat disks similar to hockey pucks. Cue sticks are used, and English can be applied, although draw and follow are impossible.

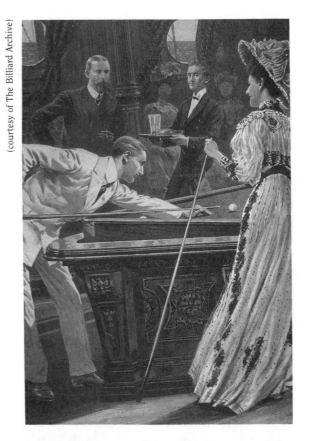

A movable inner frame that sensed the motion of the ship was the basis for this 1908 billiard table design. Notice that the outer frame is bolted to the ship's deck.

In 1908 a patent was granted for "a billiard table for ships." The table had an outer frame affixed to the deck of the ship. The inner frame, which holds the slate, is movable under the control of a complex mechanism that senses the motion of the ship and adjusts the table accordingly. The inventors claimed that it would be possible to play in any conditions other than a storm. While this table was purchased for use by a large steamship company, it was evidently not a revolutionary success, and little has since been heard of maritime billiards.

TRAINS

Train travel has always had its luxurious side. When the 1916 Chicago Cubs traveled around the country, they took a billiard table along. The accompanying photo appeared in *Sporting Records* on March 21, 1916. Not visible in the photo is a spittoon on the floor, a feature of particular importance to tobacco-chewing ball players.

AUTOMOBILES

America has had a continuing love affair with the automobile. Our attitude seems to be that

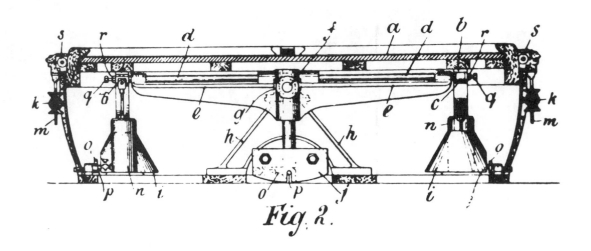

Fig. 2.

ILLUSTRATED LONDON NEWS, Dec. 26, 1908.

Chicago Cub Heinie Zimmerman takes aim at a combination shot aboard the team train in 1916. To the left of Zimmerman, chalking his cue, is Joe Tinker.

Carom billiard legend Willie Hoppe demonstrates a masse shot atop a 1934 Studebaker. The promotion, staged in Chicago, was an attempt to demonstrate the smooth ride offered by the car.

anything worth doing is worth doing in a car, including eating, sleeping, diamond cutting, and watching movies. Why not playing billiards? Willie Hoppe, the legendary carom billiards star, demonstrated some shots while riding around Chicago on top of a 1934 Studebaker. The stunt was a promotion designed to demonstrate how stable the car's ride was. Hoppe actually performed on a pocket table, shooting masse shots—no other stroke would have been visible to spectators on the street. Trolleys in Chicago experienced a wide variety of delays, but being stuck behind a moving pool table was rarely one of them.

PLANES

Strangely, it is to airborne billiards that most attention has been devoted. As soon as man learned to fly, pool players dreamed of shooting in the air.

The first actual playing of billiards aloft occurred over Detroit on December 16, 1929. Ralph Greenleaf, perhaps the greatest pool player of all time, was visiting the city to participate in the World Pocket Billiard Championship. He made four separate flights in a 12-passenger Ford trimotor, traveling about 100 mph, and had a high run of nine, playing pool on a 2½-by-5-foot table during one hour of flying. The stunt was reported to be part of a serious effort by the airlines to explore aerial entertainment, and a spokesman for Stout Air Lines, the owner of the plane, announced: "It will be necessary to provide facilities for various forms of recreation, as passengers will be spending from 3 to 24 hours a day in the air on short flights and coast-to-coast trips." More likely, the aircraft operators wanted to impress the public with the fact that flying could be a smooth experience.

Greenleaf himself must have been exhilarated by the trip. After landing, he readied himself for his tournament match that evening against Frank Taberski. Greenleaf scratched on the break, losing one point. (He drove two balls to the rail, as required, but the cue ball dropped in a pocket.) Taberski missed, and Greenleaf ran 126-and-out for 125-0 shutout, setting two world records in the process. His championship run of 126 beat the previous best of 111 (by Erwin Rudolph in the same tournament) and the two-inning victory eclipsed the former record of four (also by Rudolph). Because of the unusual circumstances of the opening scratch, the championship high run of 126 stood as a record until the length of 14.1 games was increased to 150 points more than 20 years later.

Greenleaf set off a flurry of interest in "flying" billiards. On August 17, 1930, Charles C. Peterson, the missionary of billiards, made 100 points at a discipline called Straight-Rail Billiards (a carom game) in only 28½ seconds while flying over St. Louis at 4,000 feet in a Curtis-Wright Condor. After the flight, Peterson said, "I made many difficult shots after I made the speed test. Once, when Captain Courtney tilted the plane at an angle of 30 degrees, I managed to make 10 points at Straight-Rail . . . there is a future for aerial billiards." (An optimistic view, to say the least.) The next week, Jake Schaefer, Jr., accepted a challenge from Hoppe for an airborne match at 18.2 Balkline Billiards, but there is no record of the contest ever taking place.

While no form of movable billiards has ever attained real popularity, it seems we never stop trying. The last frontier would appear to be shooting Nine-Ball aboard the space shuttle. In moving vehicles on earth, dealing with gravity is troublesome. In orbit, future astronauts will have to learn to play without it.

—"Planes, Trains, and Automobiles" by Mike Shamos. Reprint by permission of Billiards Digest.

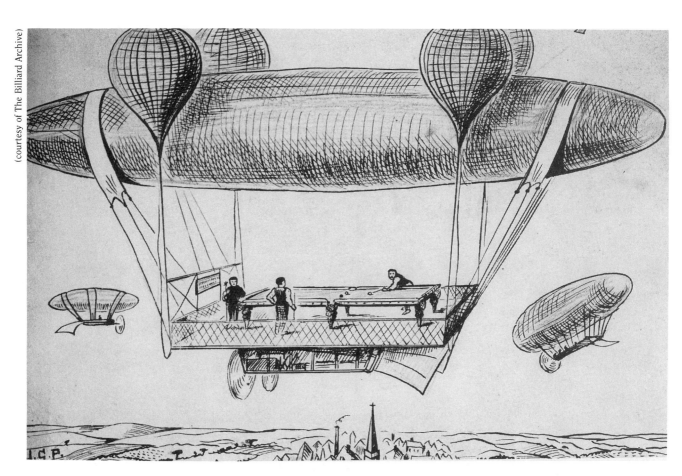

This cartoon appeared in the British publication *World of Billiards* around 1900. Penned before the Wright brothers ever took flight, it shows just how imaginative some billiard enthusiasts were.

2
Pool 101: A History of Billiards

There are many theories as to the exact origins of the family of games known as billiards. The general consensus among billiard archivists and historians is that the sport originated in the late fourteenth or early fifteenth century as an outdoor lawn game, whereby balls were rolled or pushed in the direction of other balls or targets. What is not universally agreed upon, however, is from *which* lawn game the table game version evolved. The French, English, and Italians each played lawn games with balls, and the rules and equipment in each were slightly different from the others.

Regardless, the lawn games of those days were generally enjoyed by nobility. That kings, queens, and other people of wealth and influence played these games may well have led to the invention of sticks with which to propel the balls. (Continually bending over to roll or pick up balls would likely cause a pain in the royal corset!) The earliest form of stick used to serve this purpose was made of wood and featured a flat-faced block attached to a long, narrow handle. Slightly curved at the foot, the stick was used to push or shove the balls forward.

According to billiards historian William Hendricks, in his book *The History of Billiards*, the first mention of the game being moved indoors was in 1470. An inventory list describing the accounts of King Louis XI of France made reference to the purchase of "billiard balls and billiard table for [the king's] pleasure and amusement." The table was said to have consisted of rails and a stone playing bed. The stone bed was supposedly covered with a green cloth to give the impression of grass. (Astro-turf comes to fifteenth century France?)

Billiards' popularity soared in France in the 1500s and made its way into the mansions of English nobility shortly thereafter. One of the more noted enthusiasts was Mary, Queen of Scots. Letters and documents from that time confirm that Mary had a billiard table in her prison cell while she awaited execution for her part in an assassination attempt on Queen Elizabeth I in 1588.

Billiard fever spread through the reigns of French kings Louis XIII and Louis XIV. (Their reigns encompassed roughly a century—1610-1715.) So enamored was Louis XIV with billiards that he is generally credited with spreading the game throughout Europe (as well as leading his nation into near-bankruptcy). His own private billiard room featured no fewer than 26 crystal chandeliers, 16

(courtesy of The Billiard Archive)

(courtesy of The Billiard Archive)

The beautifully ornate billiard room of Napoleon, as depicted in this early 1800s engraving. Josephine and the boys are playing carom billiards.

silver candlesticks, and two massive billiard tables. Anyone who intended to be in the favor of the king was a step ahead of the game if he or she could show competence at the billiard table.

Because billiard tables were being in-stalled in clubs and inns for use by nobility, the game eventually filtered down to the general public. The trickle-down effect also brought the sport to America in the 1700s.

Although the word *pool*, under the names Life Pool and Russian Pool, is said to have been in English rule books as early as 1819, the principal name of the game in early American billiards was Four Ball. Four Ball consisted of a cue ball and three object balls (two red and one white) on a normal six-pocket table. Points could be scored in a variety of ways: by pocketing the cue ball off an object ball; by pocketing an object ball; by pocketing a ball and having the cue ball ricochet off a cushion and into one or both of the remaining object balls; or various combinations thereof.

For several hundred years, billiards remained a game for the well-to-do. This late 1700s engraving shows a large wooden frame over the table to support candle lighting.
(courtesy of The Billiard Archive)

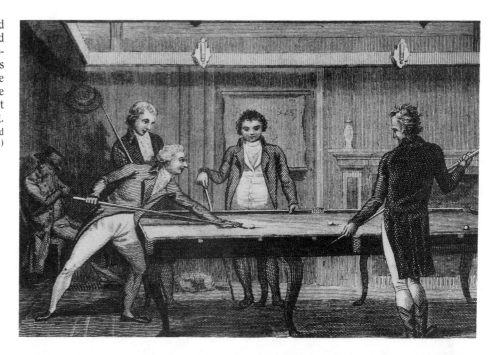

⚜ GEORGE WASHINGTON PLAYED HERE ⚜

Never one to tell a lie, George Washington—the Father of Our Country—kept close account of his money won at the billiard table.

Washington's affection for billiards is well documented in his diaries. Although his Mount Vernon home did not have enough room for a billiard table, Washington frequently visited friends whose homes did have enough room. Entries in Washington's diaries tell of his wins and losses. The most he ever lost in one day's play was one pound, ten shillings. His largest winning was said to be about $1.75.

One particular entry from June 4, 1748, states: "To cash won at billiards: one shilling, three pence." The entry further states that the "pigeon" (victim) involved was the Honorable Thomas Turner, Clerk of the Virginia House of Burgesses.

By the late 1800s, the carom games, utilizing pocketless tables, had found their way into the American billiard mainstream. The standard "Carombole" game was introduced by the French. It featured one red ball and two white cue balls—one for each player, usually distinguished by a dot on one of the cue balls. Points were scored by caroming the cue ball off one or both of the object balls. Variations required that the cue ball also strike a predetermined number of cushions during the sequence. Carom games— Straight-Rail, Balkline, and Three-Cushion— also became popular in America at the end of the nineteenth century.

With equipment at its highest level of sophistication, players of extraordinary talent began to surface. Claims of superiority spurred challenges, and with the popularity of the game at its zenith, competitive billiards in America from a public exhibition standpoint started to take shape.

The first major stakes match took place in April 1859 at Fireman's Hall in Detroit. It pitted the renowned Michael Phelan (who by then had a prosperous manufacturing company, a successful room in New York, and had authored the first two American books on billiards) against John Seereiter, the local billiard hero.

Another early nineteenth century Napoleonesque billiard scene, this time in the form of a political cartoon. The illustration is entitled "Une Partie Russe" ("A Russian Game"). The marker is pointing to the names of Napoleonic battles fought in Europe at Marengo (1800), Austerlitz (1805), and Jena (1806).

The match was Four Ball, to 2,000 points, and the purse was a then-staggering $15,000. Admission to view the match was not cheap, either—$5 per seat. More than 400 fans packed the arena, while thousands more stood outside, awaiting inning-by-inning recaps.

The four-day contest concluded with Phelan winning, 2,000-1,904. The match received extensive coverage in daily newspapers and magazines.

Phelan held the distinction of being known as the American billiard champion for three years. Then, in June 1862, the first multi-player national tournament was staged at Irving Hall in New York City. Nine of the most noted cue artists in America, including Phelan and Seereiter, assembled for a nine-day round robin championship. Irishman Dudley Kavanaugh emerged the victor. Again, the billiard competition captured the attention of the sporting world. Tournaments and high stakes matches would continue with great success well into the twentieth century.

DADDY DEAREST

Quick! Who was the "Father of American Billiards"?

Anyone who answered Willie Mosconi or Minnesota Fats is hereby sentenced to "the rack"!

American billiard pioneer Michael Phelan is generally considered the father of the game in the United States. Phelan, born in 1817, was billiards' version of Benjamin Franklin. He was a great playing talent, having won the first notable billiards stakes match over John Seereiter in 1859. Because of his flawless reputation, any tournament or match in which Phelan participated was certain to draw big crowds and good newspaper coverage.

Phelan was also an inventor and manufacturer, and his Phelan-Collender billiard table company, founded in 1840, dominated the American market for years. Phelan also patented the combination billiard cushion, as well as several unique table designs. He is even credited with being the first table maker to put ivory "diamonds" on the rails. His posh billiard room on Broadway in New York City set the trend for lavish rooms.

Away from his business, Phelan was a tireless promoter and popularizer of billiards. Not surprisingly, it was Phelan who penned the first American book on billiards, *Billiards Without a Master*, in 1859. It remains one of the best and most often quoted books on the game.

Phelan died in 1871, but his impact on the sport will last forever.

Michael Phelan—inventor, author, pool player, and businessman—is considered the Father of American Billiards.
(courtesy of the Billiard Archive)

The first official American pocket billiard tournament was held without much fanfare in 1878. Pocket billiards was not nearly as popular or accepted as the carom games. Cyrille Dion won the first American title, playing a pool game which scarcely resembles the Straight Pool discipline of later championships.

In fact, most of the games played in the early days of American billiards underwent significant changes. Both the carom games and pool became too easy for the increasingly adept professionals—and too boring to hold the public's interest.

One red ball was eliminated from the Four Ball game to make things a bit tougher. Eventually, pockets were eliminated completely, and the three-ball carom game (called Straight-Rail) was played on pocketless tables. Later still, horizontal and vertical lines were drawn on the table and rules were added to prevent a player from "gathering" the three balls in a small area along a rail. Through "gathering," a player could literally score hundreds of points and never move the three balls more than a few feet. By adding the lines (thus, the name change to Balkline), players were allowed only a small number of points within each "balk area" before being required to move the balls to another area.

Balkline emerged as the main American professional billiard game in the early 1900s, with champions like Jake Schaefer, Sr., and Willie Hoppe dominating the game.

By the late 1920s and into the 1930s, the carom and pocket games underwent yet another change—this time for good. Three-Cushion Billiards became *the* carom game, while 14.1 Continuous emerged as the choice of pocket billiard professionals. (To score in Three-Cushion, the shooting player's cue ball must strike one of the two object balls and

(courtesy of The Billiard Archive)

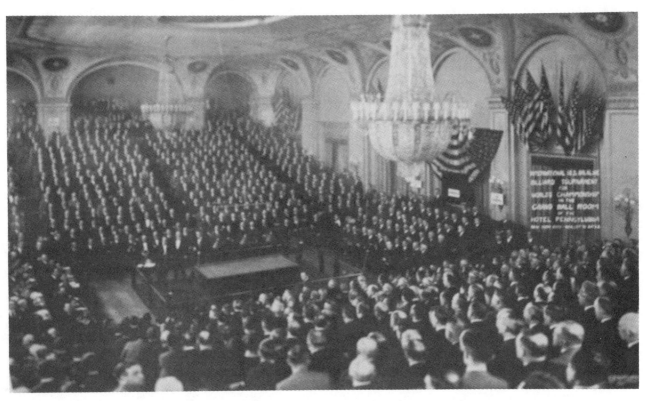

THIS IS POOL?

During most of the sport's early years in America, pool took a back seat to Four Ball—a game combining pocketing and carom skills. The first-ever billiards tournament in America, held in New York City in 1862, was a nine-player Four Ball event. It received much fanfare and newspaper coverage.

Almost unnoticeably, the first American *pool* tournament took place in 1878, also in New York City. It was won by Cyrille Dion, who defeated Gothard Wahlstrom, 11–7, for the title. The score may seem a bit strange, considering that today's top players routinely post runs of 100 consecutive balls.

Were the first pool players *that* bad?

Not at all. The game played in the first pool championship was called Fifteen Ball Pool. The rules were relatively simple and are still listed in the Billiard Congress of America's *Official Rules and Record Book*. One rack constitutes a "frame." The numerical value of the ball pocketed is awarded to the shooter—i.e., the 15-ball is worth 15 points. Since the balls numbered 1 through 15 total 120 points, the first player to accumulate 61 points wins the frame.

In the pool championship of 1878, the format was based on best-of-21 frames. Thus Dion, by virtue of his 11-frame to 7-frame decision, was America's first *pool* champion.

---

three cushions, in any order, before striking the second object ball.)

The changes added new excitement to the games, and with them, two of the most legendary players of all time emerged—Willie Hoppe and Ralph Greenleaf. Hoppe, polished and gentlemanly, dominated the Balkline and Three-Cushion divisions for nearly 20 years. Greenleaf, handsome and charismatic, accumulated 14 world pocket billiard titles.

By the late 1940s, however, pocket billiards (which was under the spell of Willie Mosconi and other exceptional talents such as Jimmy Caras, Erwin Rudolph, Andrew Ponzi, and Irving Crane) had begun to surpass the carom games in popularity.

Then came one of the billiard industry's cyclical "crashes." The late 1950s saw poolrooms across the country closing their doors and table sales hitting rock bottom. The bust period was ended with a resounding boom, however, when *The Hustler* hit movie screens in 1961. After a half dozen years, though, the popularity of billiards in America swooned again.

From the mid-seventies to the early eighties, pool's popularity was once again on the rebound. The release of the movie *The Color of Money* in 1986 lit the fuse for pool's latest surge, but many factors point to an extended run of good fortune for the game. First, the professional side of the game—despite having to fight for acceptance against big-money sports like golf and tennis—grows stronger with each passing year. The number of poolrooms in America is growing steadily, and the rooms are catering to a broader clientele than at any other time. Also, the continued growth of grass-roots tavern pool leagues is adding legions of dedicated players to pool's ranks. Finally, one recent sports survey went so far as to tab billiards as "the sport of the '90s!"

The *new* modern era of billiards is upon us and promises to grow and flourish in the years to come.

EVOLUTION OF EQUIPMENT

While billiards equipment has changed very little in the twentieth century, the first 400 years of the game's existence saw so many alterations it's no wonder historians have had such a difficult time piecing this puzzle together.

Changes in equipment begat changes in the nature of the games themselves, and changes in the game in England did not necessarily result in adjustments in France and/or America.

TABLES

The first definitive notation of a table made for the express purpose of playing billiards was in 1470. The table, commissioned by France's King Louis XI, was said to include a bed of stone, a cloth covering, and a hole in the middle of the playfield, into which balls were driven.

Later, pockets were moved to the outer edges of the playfield, and most featured six pockets—one at each corner, and one along each long rail. As billiards in the seventeenth century was still evolving from its outdoor forefathers, an ivory arch and upright target (called a "king") were placed near the center of the table. Each player had his own cue ball and could score points by sending his ball through the arch, or "port," or by making contact with the "king" *without* knocking it over.

Until the middle of the eighteenth century, billiard tables were crudely constructed, with little concern given to the stability of the piece. The bed was nothing more than a thin wooden board, and the inner construction did little to keep the board from warping.

By the early 1800s, accomplished cabinetmakers were beginning to produce solidly constructed billiard tables. While the bed was generally still made from wood, greater efforts were made to build and secure the bed through the use of various dried hardwoods and dowels. Slate beds followed shortly thereafter, and, due to the weight of slate, the inner construction of billiard tables became even more complex and substantial.

Later in the nineteenth century, table manufacturers began experimenting with gulleys and channels through which balls could be returned to a catch at one end of the table. Until that time, balls had been held in nets or traps attached to each pocket.

Dimensions of the tables varied, seemingly at the whimsy of the designer. Still, most tables were approximately twice as long as they were wide. Today, standard pool tables vary from 6 feet in length to 10 feet. As a rule of thumb, pocket openings can accommodate two pool balls set side by side. Carom tables are generally 5 feet wide by 10 feet long.

CUSHIONS

As tables became more advanced, the need for reliable reactions of billiard balls off the cushions became more obvious. The level of play, it was surmised, would never reach great heights unless players could come to expect consistent play from the cushions.

In the early days of billiard tables, the cushions were nothing more than short walls of wood. Lining the walls with leather failed to produce acceptable results, so cloth was wrapped around the cushions and stuffed with hair or cotton. Further experimentation has been said to include cushions blown up with compressed air.

Crude rubber from India made its way onto billiard cushions around 1835, but the material turned rock-hard when the room temperature dropped. Remedies included detachable rails which could be warmed near an open fire before play, and hot irons with which to heat the cushions. Conversely, in excessive heat, the rubber softened to mush and needed to be iced.

Vulcanization, the process of chemically

treating rubber so it can retain its elasticity regardless of temperature, changed the billiard cushion for good around 1845. Combinations of the vulcanized rubber, leather, and cork helped make the billiard table cushions reliable and consistent. Because so many of the billiard games at that time required caroms, the new material helped the quality of play soar almost immediately.

(courtesy of *Billiards Digest*)

Not even a "Hun gas attack" could kill the lively cushions on this billiard table, insisted a World War I-vintage advertisement for Goodrich billiard cushions, which were made of vulcanized rubber.

BALLS

The majority of billiard balls in use during the game's early years were made of wood. It was easily turned and shaped and was inexpensive. Ivory balls, formed from the tusks of elephants, were in use as early as 1627. While preferred by most billiard enthusiasts, ivory balls were relatively scarce. Only the wealthy could afford the material.

While beautiful to look at, ivory billiard balls were never very dependable. For starters, the elephant tusks had to be properly seasoned—sometimes as long as two years. The gelatin in tusks, which gives the material its glossy polish, was also a source of moisture. Unless the tusk was dried properly, excessive temperature changes could cause the mate-

rial to fracture or even split. Ivory also tended to lose its shape easily.

With the purchase of a set of ivory billiard balls came elaborate instructions regarding their delicate nature. Because the balls were liable to absorb moisture, players were warned not to hold the spheres in their hands for any length of time. A "set of ivories," as they were called, needed to be painstakingly broken in. Owners were advised to keep the balls in a place of even temperature and to strike them lightly for several months until they became acclimated to the environment.

Still, ivory billiard balls all but entirely replaced wooden balls early in the nineteenth century. As the demand for the balls increased, so too did the number of slaughtered elephants. Curiously, the overriding concern at the time was not the shameless treatment of the elephants, but the safety of those who tracked the animals to their deaths.

With the game's popularity on the rise, and demand for equipment following suit, the billiard industry launched a search for an alternative to ivory. In 1868, a chemist named John Wesley Hyatt discovered celluloid, a durable plastic that could be molded to near-perfect roundness and was not affected by temperature extremes. (A collective sigh of relief was said to have been heard from the herds in Tanzania!) A few years later, the process was fine-tuned to the cast-phenolic method still employed today.

CUES

The most obvious, and dramatic, change in equipment has been the development of the cue stick. As early as 1600, the object used to shove balls forward on a billiard table was the *mace*. The head of the mace was wide and flat-faced. The heel of the wooden block was curved slightly, and a long stick was extended from it. This allowed players to stand erect and slide the head of the mace along the playing surface.

(courtesy of *Billiards Digest*)

Considering that the average elephant tusk produces roughly five ivory billiard balls, the number of animals slaughtered for this pile must have been staggering.

As players sought more precision, a more narrow macehead attached to a straight stick was introduced in the mid-1600s. For even more precision, and to aid with shots near the cushion, accomplished players turned the mace around and shot with the tail end of the stick. By the turn of the seventeenth century, the cue as a separate piece of equipment was in use. Although women continued to use the mace until the end of the nineteenth century, men only used it when aiming their cues at hard-to-reach shots. Thus, the mace actually served as the first mechanical bridge.

Developed strictly as a matter of convenience, the two-piece tapered cue stick came into use before 1900. Although the cue stick has not undergone any significant changes since then, some of the cues manufactured at the turn of the century featured wide grips that tapered off slightly to the butt end. The "fishing pole" style didn't last, but the practice of garnishing the butt of the cue with elaborate inlays and designs was prevalent even then.

The 1800s proved to be the century during which billiards went through its most dramatic changes—alterations that would eventually thrust the game into its current state. Perhaps the most important change, the invention of the leather cue tip, is credited to a jailed French infantry captain named Mingaud. As the story goes, Mingaud was imprisoned in Paris at the beginning of the nineteenth century. The prison had a billiard table, to which Mingaud devoted all of his time. How this guy came to discover that, by mounting a patch of leather to the tip of the cue stick, he could impart a significant amount of spin to the cue ball remains a mystery. What *is* known, however, is that Mingaud's fascination with billiards was *intense*. At the end of his prison term, he actually asked for more time in jail so that he might complete his study of the game!

Chalk, which added to the tip's power over the cue ball, was also in wide use by the 1820s. The first known cubes of chalk were white. By the mid-1800s, most of the ways in which a cue tip could affect the cue ball were pretty widely known.

ODDITIES AND SHORTCUTS

Inventors have always had a reputation for being a tad eccentric, concocting elaborate and oftentimes complicated gadgets and devices, spurred by the notion that these products will make our lives easier. Here are a handful of fascinating "improvements" on standard pool equipment, all patented between 1867 and 1915. The majority of the inventions revolve around the cue stick—either cues that virtually shoot by themselves, or bridge-hand guides to improve aim and execution.

(courtesy of The Billiard Archive)

◄ Dow McClain's "Home Hygienic Pool Cue," patented in 1901.

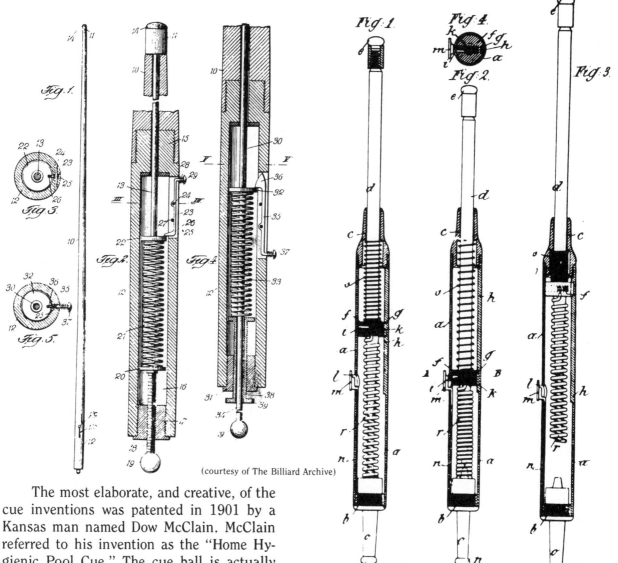

(courtesy of The Billiard Archive)

The most elaborate, and creative, of the cue inventions was patented in 1901 by a Kansas man named Dow McClain. McClain referred to his invention as the "Home Hygienic Pool Cue." The cue ball is actually "shot" through the cue by compressed air—which is supplied by the shooter! McClain claimed that, "aside from the agreeable entertainment derived from [the cue], it will be conducive to healthful and correct breathing, inasmuch as it will necessitate deep and hygienic exercise of the lungs."

The more standard cue improvements of the day were those cues of the spring-driven variety. The earliest of these spring-loaded cues was patented in 1901. A Frenchman named Henri Victor Beaufils claimed that his mechanical cue was a vast improvement over previously offered models. Not only was Beaufils's cue spring-propelled, but the force of the stroke could be adjusted.

Spring-propelled cues were the rage in the early 1900s. Most had more working parts than a Swiss watch!

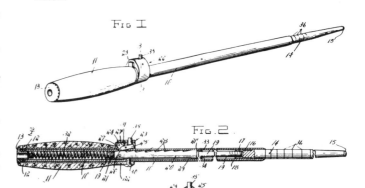

William Hall of New Jersey, in 1909, and James J. Teague of Holbrook, Arizona, in 1915, added new wrinkles to the spring-loaded cue market. Both cues were essentially hollowed tubes with a coil spring which, when engaged, would thrust the sliding sleeve of the cue forward. The cues featured set screws, springs, plungers, triggers, and ratchet teeth! Can't understand how they didn't catch on!

The predecessors to the self-propelled cues, in terms of convenience and efficiency, were the cue guides of the late 1800s. Several came in the form of rings, upon which cue-guiding channels were attached. One of the simpler devices was a sleeve for the shaft, around which you'd wrap your bridge fingers, allowing the cue to slide easily back and forth.

But the most bizarre aid was the "cue support" patented by Josiah Miller of Mansfield, Ohio, in 1899. Miller's creation was a hollowed sphere, inside which a cube of chalk could be housed. In operation, the hollow sphere was grasped in the bridge hand and placed in position for shooting. The shaft of the cue slid through the ring at the top of the device!

The mechanical bridge head also underwent its fair share of improvements. One par-

ticularly impressive idea was a bridge head, patented in 1867, which utilized five spool-like rollers. When attempting a difficult-to-reach shot, you simply slid the shaft back and forth on one of the rollers.

Anyone who has attempted to rack balls for a game of Eight-Ball knows how difficult it is to remove the triangle without disturbing the perfectly frozen balls. Thomas Madigan's patented 1914 triangle solved that problem—briefly, I'm sure. Madigan's triangle actually featured hinges, which allowed the racker to lift the front of the triangle without risk of upsetting the balls. (You just don't see too many of those racks around anymore!)

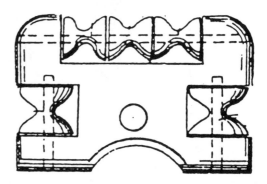

Improvements on the mechanical bridge head have abounded through the years. One of the more logical inventions was this, a wooden device with five rolling spools, patented in 1867.
(courtesy of Joe Newell)

CUE REST.

Patented Nov. 3, 1896.

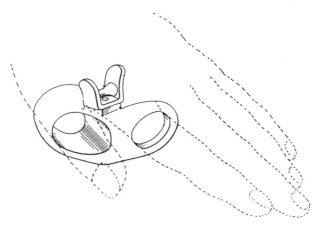

(courtesy of Joe Newell)

Fig 1.

Fig 2.

Fig 3.

Fig 4.

Fig. 1

Fig. 2

BILLIARD CUE.

Patented Nov. 27, 1894.

Learning to form a proper bridge for guiding the cue is one of the game's tougher challenges. As a result, a host of ring-like support devices have been patented over the years. Some were very clever, but few lasted.

Because home billiard tables tend to take up so much room, manufacturers have spent years developing tables that can be converted to standard pieces of furniture. One such attempt in 1899 produced a three-layer extravaganza. In its complete upright position, the piece was a nicely cushioned settee with two small tables. When you wanted to take a nap, you simply let the bed down. Had enough rest? Lower the top of the arrangement, and chalk up!

The combination table, displayed in a magazine called *The Designer*, was suggested for the summer cottage, "where an extra bed is frequently needed for an unexpected guest, and a billiard table is always a welcome addition."

It's hard to imagine how the hinged triangle failed to make it big! The concept, developed in 1914, was noble, but demand for the product simply wasn't there.
(courtesy of Joe Newell)

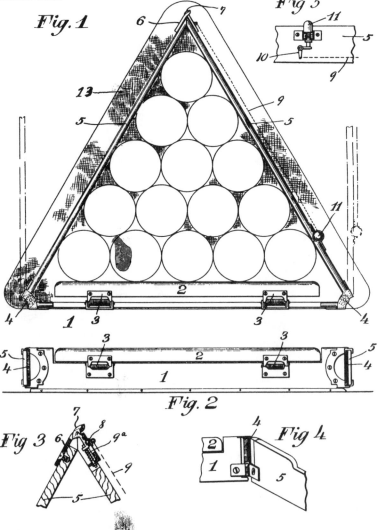

Fig. 1

Fig 5

Fig. 2

Fig 3

Fig 4

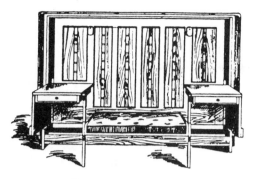

No. 1.—Settee and Stands.

No. 2.—Bed and Dressing Glass.

No. 3.—Billiard Table.

Here's a novel idea—a turn-of-the-century combination settee/bed/billiard table.

El "Cozy Home"

The combination dining room table/pool table has been one of the more enduring table conversion ideas.

SIGNIFICANT MOMENTS IN BILLIARD HISTORY

1350–1450	Period during which lawn games resembling billiards were thought to start.
1470	First definitive mention of the existence of a billiard table, noted in the inventory of France's King Louis XI.
1588	Mary, Queen of Scots, whiles away the time preceding her execution by playing billiards.
1660–1690	Period during which use of the narrow end of the mace for the purpose of executing shots is introduced.
1710	Billiards reaches the American colonies.
1740	The cue establishes itself as separate from the mace.
1792	King Louis XVI and Marie Antoinette engage in a game of billiards on the eve of the French Revolution.
1818	Captain Mingaud, an imprisoned French soldier, invents and perfects the use of a leather tip for the billiard cue, through which spin may be imparted onto the cue ball.
1835	England's John Thurston introduces the slate billiard table bed.
1845	Thurston patents billiard table cushions using the newly discovered vulcanized rubber.
1859	The first high stakes challenge match, pitting Michael Phelan and John Seereiter in Four Ball, takes place at Fireman's Hall in Detroit.
1862	The first major tournament, featuring nine of America's best Four Ball players, is held at Irving Hall in New York City.
1868	Isaac and John Wesley Hyatt develop the celluloid billiard ball, thus eliminating the need for ivory balls.
1878	The first American pocket billiard championship is held at Union Square in New York City.
1906	Willie Hoppe wins his first Balkline championship, defeating champion Maurice Vignaux of France in Paris.
1919	Ralph Greenleaf wins the first of 14 world pocket billiard titles.
1928	Three-Cushion billiards replaces Balkline as the carom game of champions.
1941	Willie Mosconi wins the first of 15 world pocket billiard titles.
1961	*The Hustler*, starring Paul Newman, opens in theaters across America, igniting a "boom" period for pocket billiards.
1978	Nine-Ball replaces 14.1 Continuous as the game of choice at professional pocket billiard tournaments.
1986	*The Color of Money* spurs another resurgence of pocket billiards.
1989	Fashionable, plush poolrooms emerge, setting the stage for billiards in the nineties.

3
Pool Notables

FAMOUS HOBBYISTS

The history of the cue games is freckled with tales of famous hobbyists; no less than kings, queens, and presidents have confessed addictions to the games of the green baize.

King Louis XIV of France and Mary, Queen of Scots, were notable devotees, the latter to the point of obsession. But a lesser known fanatic, whose thirst for "yet another game" led to claims of scandal and cries of outrage, was none other than the sixth President of the United States, John Quincy Adams.

Actually, Adams's reputation as a hustler was evident even before he took office in 1825. A Northerner from Massachusetts, Adams finished second to Andrew Jackson in the regular election. Because there were four candidates (Adams, Jackson, Henry Clay, and William H. Crawford) on the ballot, however, no one candidate received a majority of the electoral votes. The House of Representatives had to select the president, and Clay (a lifelong Jackson-basher) threw his support to Adams. In turn, Adams named Clay his Secretary of State. Naturally, Jackson denounced the Adams-Clay merger as a "corrupt bargain." The opposing groups decided to con-

solidate, and frustration became the keynote of the Adams administration.

But Adams's big problems began with the installation of a billiard table in the White House. Although Adams insisted that the $14,000 Congressional appropriation for new furnishings had "all been made with an eye to the strictest economy," the following items turned up on a list submitted to Representative Stephen Van Rensselaer: billiard table, $50.00; cloth and work, $43.44; cues, $5.00; and billiard balls, $6.00.

Adams's opponents were incensed and immediately turned the purchase into a national issue. One Southern representative inquired, "Was it ever intended by Congress that public money should be applied to the purchase of gaming tables and gambling furniture?"

Newspaper editorials also pounced on the story. Wrote one paper: "When we find the fathers and matrons of our country engaged in persuading young men from practices which lead to destruction, we greatly fear that the too frequent answer will be, 'Why, the President plays billiards!' To this, there will be no answer."

Suffice to say, the image associated with the game was not terribly complimentary in

1825. In fact, the game was banned in many states.

Perhaps the most recognized billiard fanatic was Samuel Langhorn Clemens, better known as Mark Twain. Twain, born just six years after Adams left the White House, was known to spend countless hours at his pocket table, playing a discipline known as English Billiards, a game using only three balls and combining the skills of carom and pocket billiards. In fact, several of Twain's homes (he owned homes in the United States and abroad) included a room equipped with a billiard table, the most noted being the third-floor billiard area of his 19-room mansion in Hartford, Connecticut.

The celebrated author was also an avid fan of the professional game. He adopted Willie Hoppe as his personal favorite and was often a spectator at championship matches played in New York City.

Twain often wrote on the subject of billiards and produced several hilarious anecdotes about being hustled and about his preference for substandard equipment. The use of crooked cues, chipped balls, and a slanted table, Twain surmised, made the game more amusing and led to more admiration for anyone who could master the game despite such obvious handicaps.

The most impressive endorsement Twain gave the game, however, was in the context of a letter he wrote to a friend. Said Twain: "The billiard table is better than the doctors. I walk not less than ten miles with a cue in my hand, and the walking is not the whole of the

❦ HERE'S TO YOUR HEALTH ❧

One tack taken by the billiard industry in its fight against the notion that the game was synonymous with gambling and evil was to promote the sport as healthy exercise.

Among other things, billiards was touted as a means through which people could avoid gallstones, cure insomnia, squelch indigestion, prevent appendicitis, and soothe rheumatism. Now *there's* a trick shot!

(courtesy of The Billiard Archive)

◀ At the turn of the century, billiards was touted as being a great form of exercise. Some poolrooms were even billed as health spas.

exercise, nor the most health-giving part of it. I think, through the multitude of positions and attitudes, it brings into play every muscle of the body and exercises them all."

Not all famous enthusiasts were high-profile public figures. America's first Nobel Prize scientist (1907), Albert Abraham Michelson, the University of Chicago Physicist generally associated with measuring the speed of light, was a devout billiardist. Michelson was said to have played carom billiards every single day at the exact same time—noon. Even at the age of 75 (Michelson

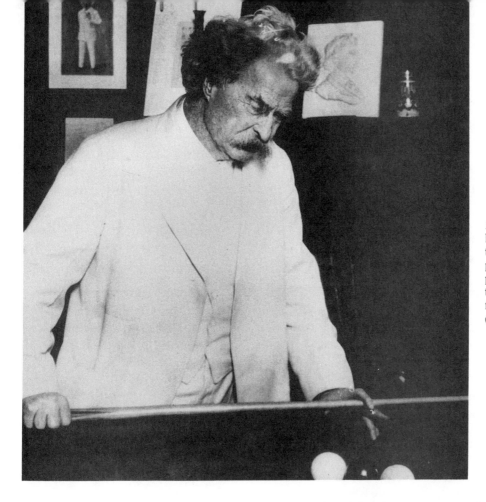

Mark Twain was an avid billiardist, and he often traveled to New York to see professional championship play. Willie Hoppe was said to have been Twain's favorite young player.
(courtesy of The Billiard Archive)

died at 78 in 1931), Michelson was said to be a topflight Straight-Rail player.

While most famous billiard hobbyists did little more than sing praises for the game, modern-day comedian David Brenner has taken his love for pool a step further. The Philadelphia native, who claims to have spent the better part of his youth playing pocket billiards, has opened a posh new billiard room on New York City's trendy Upper West Side. Amsterdam Billiards, a 30-table second-floor room in what had previously been a bowling center, may be the first room to call an established celebrity its owner.

Who knows? Maybe show business and sports stars will grow tired of opening the seemingly obligatory restaurant, and the United States will boast a string of celebrity billiard rooms!

America's first Nobel Prize–winning physicist, Albert ▶ Michelson, played billiards every day at noon.

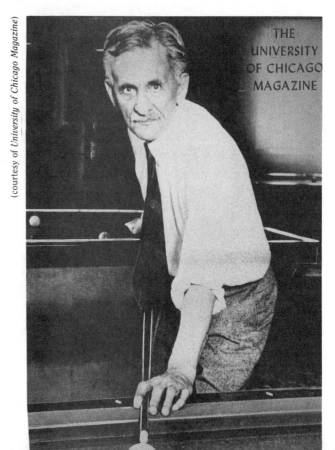

(courtesy of University of Chicago Magazine)

THE UNIVERSITY OF CHICAGO MAGAZINE

✂THE GREATEST EVER?✂

Regardless of the sport, the fastest way to stir up heated discussion is to pose the question, "Who was the greatest ever?"

In pocket billiards, that question is still cause for great debate. The general consensus is that the finalists are Willie Mosconi and Ralph Greenleaf. Greenleaf, a child prodigy from Monmouth, Illinois, reigned over the pocket billiard world from 1919–1938. During that time, the classy showman won 14 world pocket billiard titles. Mosconi won the first of his 15 world championships in 1941 and dominated the sport until his retirement in 1957.

Although their careers intertwined only briefly in the late thirties, Greenleaf and Mosconi did spend the summer of 1934 together, touring the South. Greenleaf, 38 at the time, won the majority of the early matches against his 21-year-old opponent, but Mosconi held his own in the later exhibitions. After 107 matches, Greenleaf had won 57 to Mosconi's 50.

Perhaps the greatest legacy of Mosconi's career are his high runs. The Philadelphia native still holds the recognized mark of 526 balls at an exhibition in Springfield, Ohio, in 1954. The run was achieved on a 4-by-8-foot table. Even more impressive may be Mosconi's 356-ball run on a 5-by-10-foot table in Wilmington, North Carolina. Incredibly Mosconi posted four 300-plus runs on the merciless 10-footers, which were standard for championship play in that era.

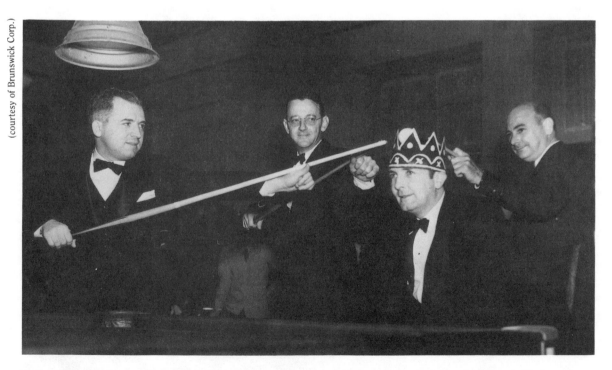

(courtesy of Brunswick Corp.)

Pocket billiard stars spent year after frustrating year trying, unsuccessfully, to dethrone 14-time world champion Greenleaf. Pictured here are (left to right) Andrew Ponzi, Joe Diehl, Ralph Greenleaf, and Benny Allen.

Greenleaf never matched Mosconi's propensity for high runs, but exhibition play was never his style. Greenleaf was flamboyant and a great admirer of the good life. It's been said that Greenleaf, a natural talent, never practiced a day in his life. He was, indeed, the "Babe Ruth" of pocket billiards.

(courtesy of *Billiards Digest*)

Stylish and confident, Mosconi personified the word *class*.

PLAYERS PAST AND PRESENT

When I was growing up, I viewed the professional players I'd seen and heard about with reverence and awe. They were my idols. I viewed pro pool players the same way kids today view rock and roll stars. I wanted to be just like those pool players.

The biggest names when I was growing up were Willie Mosconi and Ralph Greenleaf. I saw Mosconi play plenty of times, but Greenleaf was more of a mysterious legend to me. I never saw him play, but the stories I'd heard about his phenomenal ability would put me into a trance.

Greenleaf was from pool's Golden Era (1920–1940), just a tad before my time. Mosconi was in his prime during the latter part of that period. Other legends from that age were fellows like Andrew Ponzi, Erwin Rudolph, Frank Taberski, and Jimmy Caras. Mosconi's career carried into the late fifties, and Caras came out of retirement to win the Billiard Congress of America U.S. Open title in 1967.

There weren't many tournaments in those days. World championships were decided in great part by "challenge matches" between the recognized champion and a top contender—like boxing. But what few major multi-player events there were, I got to see my share. There were six-man and eight-man round robin tournaments in New York City. My father used to take me to watch the best players in the world. Naturally, I was like the proverbial kid in a candy store. I couldn't get enough. I sat in the stands for hours and hours, watching as many matches as I could.

All of the championship tournaments back then were Straight Pool. Straight Pool

Greenleaf was an astonishing natural talent who loathed practice and loved nights on the town with his vaudevillian wife Amelia, known in the 1920s as "Princess Nai-Tai-Tai, the Oriental Nightingale."

Irving "The Deacon" Crane epitomized the qualities of a classic Straight Pool player. He was inordinately patient, calculating, and unflappable.

takes patience, composure, and more patience. Players must be reserved. Back then, the players' demeanors—both at the table and in the chair—were a reflection of the game. Straight Pool is also methodical. You can't end the game early. You must score 150 or 200 points, and that's not something you can fly through.

Most of the greats from 20 to 30 years ago were men who played the game on an even keel. They weren't overly emotional, and many of them were defensive-minded players. Irving Crane is a prime example.

Crane, a Cadillac salesman from Rochester, New York, was nicknamed "The Deacon," and with good reason. Crane, now 77 years

old and still living in Rochester, is tall and very thin. A man of few words away from the table, Crane was a man of *no* words *at* the table. He always wore the same stoic expression regardless of the score. He was a thinking man's pool player, constantly calculating his strategy. He may well have been the finest safety player I ever saw in Straight Pool.

Not that Crane couldn't run balls, too. In the championship match at the 1966 Billiard Congress of America U.S. Open, Crane traded safeties with his opponent, Joe Balsis, for several innings, then calmly ran 150-and-out to win the title!

Perhaps the most amazing thing about Irving Crane's career was its longevity. In each of four consecutive decades, Crane won at least one world championship. His first title came in 1942. He also won world crowns in '56, '66, '68, '70, and '72. Four of his world titles were won after his 53rd birthday. That's impressive!

The fifties and sixties also featured stars like Arthur "Babe" Cranfield, Onofrio Lauri, and Jimmy Moore.

Moore, called "Cowboy," was more flamboyant than most Straight Pool players. He wore boots, a Stetson hat, and a string tie. Another trademark of Jimmy Moore's was his "slip stroke," the act of "slipping" his grip hand back on the cue just before stroking, a backswing without moving the cue. Moore's game, like Mosconi's, combined a perfect blend of offense and defense.

Another great player was the late Luther Lassiter. Luther was different. He grew up a big-time money player, gambling mostly at Nine-Ball in places like Norfolk, Virginia, De-

(courtesy of Billiards Digest)

A player who excelled both offensively and defensively in Straight Pool was Jimmy Moore. Here Moore (right) plays against Willie Mosconi at the 1953 World's Invitational in San Francisco.

Luther Lassiter was an offensive machine. Although his main game was Nine-Ball, Lassiter was so talented he beat the very best players at Straight Pool as well.

troit, and anywhere else players were betting high. Basically, Lassiter played Straight Pool for fun, but he was such a great player that he could beat virtually anybody at that game, too.

At tournaments, Lassiter was a sight. He was never without an ailment—sinus problems, stomach problems, puffed-up eyes. He'd moan his way right through the winner's bracket, beating everyone handily. He was something.

Personally, I was pretty successful against Lassiter. Twice I defeated him in the

championship match at the BCA U.S. Open, in 1970 and 1973. While I looked on with awe when watching these players from the bleachers, I have to admit that when I began competing *against* them, I was less than reverent. I was a very confident young player.

I'll never forget the first tournament in which I came up against the greats. In 1964 (I was still a teenager), I was invited to compete in a 16-player round robin event at the Elgin Country Club in Elgin, Illinois. The tournament was called the "TV Tournament of Champions," and the matches were taped and run as a 13-week series on television. Chris Schenkel and Willie Mosconi did the commentary.

The format consisted of Straight Pool matches to 75 points, which is hardly an equitable test for pros, but, as always, television calls the shots! The tables were fitted with tight 4½-inch pockets. Anyone who ran 75-and-out would receive a $500 bonus, but these tables were tough!

I wasn't scheduled for an early game, and I remember watching the others struggle in their matches. I mean, these were the 16 greatest pool players in the world (well, 15 and me). I said to Crane, who I had only met once or twice, "Gee, how come these guys are missing so much?" Irv just said, "Son, wait until you get out there. Then come back and ask me that question."

It just so happens I played very well in my first match and ended up with the high run of the tournament—59. I couldn't resist going back to Crane with the same question. He probably thought I was a bit too cocky. Irv had the last laugh, though. He finished first, and I came in second.

In the late sixties, when I started playing in more pro tournaments, Joe Balsis was my idol. I really liked his game. He played great offense—strong and gutsy. If Joe needed 28 balls for the championship, he was simply going to find a way to run 28. It was a dead cinch.

The players who have solid games are obvious, because they can withstand long layoffs and return to near-peak performance levels. Balsis had that type of game. He gave up pool for 17 years, from 1947 to 1963, then

(photo by Billie Billing)

The best player of the eighties was probably Mike Sigel, who knows the game inside and out and plays every game at the highest level of skill.

returned and was one of the game's dominant players for nearly a decade more. Five times he reached the BCA U.S. Open finals, winning twice. On three occasions, Balsis won the World All-Around title. After another sabbatical from pool, Balsis returned to finish third at the Professional Pool Players Association World Open in 1982.

Amazingly, some of the best players from those days never competed in tournaments. In truth, tournament prize money wasn't that great, and many players didn't think tournaments were worth exposing themselves to. Guys like Eddie Taylor, Marshall Carpenter, and Johnny Vevis preferred anonymity.

About the only time these "road players," as they were called, came out of the closet was for the annual hustler's jamboree in Johnston City, Illinois. For one three-week period every year from 1966 to the mid-seventies, the best gambling pool players in the world descended on this seed-of-a-town in southern Illinois for a series of tournaments called The World All-Around Championships. The competition consisted of a Nine-Ball tournament, a One-Pocket tournament, and a Straight Pool tournament. Then the winners of each division would play a three-man round robin final for the all-around title.

While the tournament featured great competition, the real action revolved around the back room. Matches for big money took place in the back room of Paul and Georgie Jansco's poolroom in Johnston City. Guys matched up playing any kind of pool game with outrageous spots and outlandish handicaps. One-handed Nine-Ball, where you can hold the cue with just one hand, Bank Pool, One-Pocket . . . *anything*. Even Minnesota Fats, never noted for his tournament record, showed up in Johnston City.

I went there a few times, but never to enter the tournament. I just watched. It was a true experience—a subculture unto itself.

(photo by Michael E. Panozzo)

Earl Strickland was *born* to play Nine-Ball. An emotional player who thrives on adrenaline and the roar of the crowds, Strickland is second only to Sigel in the most titles won in the past 10 years.

Today, there aren't as many "hidden" talents. With so many tournaments being run, and decent prize money being offered, the best players are all out in the open.

The players today are much different from the guys I saw when I was growing up. A lot of that has to do with the change in games. As I said before, the players tend to be extensions of the games they play. Straight Pool players are more reserved. The Nine-Ball players are more flamboyant and play more on emotion and adrenaline. There are more peaks and valleys in a Nine-Ball game, and emotion and momentum come into play.

Earl Strickland is cut from the Nine-Ball cloth. When he's on a roll, he just races around the table. He's a spectacular shot maker and doesn't shy away from many opportunities to run out. David Howard is the same way. He's noted for his explosive break shots, as well as for peculiar body twists and expressions he displays while playing.

The best of the best, however, are Mike Sigel, Allen Hopkins, Buddy Hall, and Nick Varner—all contemporaries of mine and, not coincidentally, players who grew up playing Straight Pool.

Sigel is a flashy, stylish left-hander who has superior confidence in his ability. He plays all games well and has exceptional knowledge about the sport. Hopkins is not as flashy, but his vast knowledge puts him on the same par.

Nick Varner has always been a top-notch player, but in 1989 he set the standard by which all future champions will have to measure their success. The little man from Owensboro, Kentucky, won everything in sight in 1989—including *eight* Men's Professional Billiard Association titles!

Buddy Hall, among the best Nine-Ball players during the eighties, is somewhat of a contradiction to the Nine-Ball stereotype. Another Kentuckian, Hall is in no rush to move around the table. Methodically he stalks the balls, pumping them into pockets with

(courtesy of *Billiards Digest*)

Little Nick Varner proved that life begins at forty by winning a record *eight* major titles in 1989!

his compact, pistonlike stroke. You won't see Buddy Hall make a lot of spectacular shots, in great part because he plays position with such precision that spectacular shots aren't necessary.

Although there are hundreds of players who compete in professional pool tournaments, it is my contention that there are fewer than 10 *great* players today—with Sigel, Hopkins, Varner, Hall, Jim Rempe, Efren Reyes of the Philippines, and myself among the 10. Years ago, there were maybe 25 who could be classified as great. Still, the great players of today could have played on equal par with the great pool players of any era.

NICKNAMES

MY FAVORITE POOL NICKNAMES

Pool has long been noted for its colorful characters, guys who've been everywhere, seen everything, and played everyone. They spin marvelous yarns of their adventures as modern-day gunslingers.

⚞ POOL GOES HOLLYWOOD ⚟

Hollywood's association with the sport of pocket billiards goes well beyond the trick shots and broken thumbs of *The Hustler* and *The Color of Money*. As early as 1915, pocket billiards was popping up on film reels around the country—sometimes as the main subject, other times as a blip of a scene.

Some of the earliest movie scenes of pool were in the form of shorts that preceded the feature films. Generally, the shorts featured the game's premier players displaying their talents on the green baize. Stars like Willie Hoppe, Willie Mosconi, Irving Crane, Andrew Ponzi, and trick-shot legend Charlie Peterson helped to put the sport in a very positive light.

Pool as comic relief was a common theme in early Hollywood productions. W. C. Fields, an accomplished pool player (and hustler), Laurel and Hardy, and the Three Stooges broke audiences up with their slapstick antics around the billiard table. Billiards also served as sport for such cue-wielding luminaries as Jonathan Winters and Jack Klugman (in an old "Twilight Zone" episode), Frank Sinatra and Montgomery Clift (in *From Here to Eternity*), Shirley MacLaine (twice! in *Irma La Douce* and *The Bliss of Mrs. Blossom*), Clara Bow and Charles Ruggles (in *Her Wedding Night*), and Pinocchio (in the Disney animated film).

For the most part, though, *serious* pool was never a consideration, nor was preparing the actors or actresses to appear at all learned in the art of playing billiards. Few tinsel-types knew the first thing about holding a cue, much less stroking one.

Some stars developed (or had already established) a true passion for the games. Fred Astaire reportedly practiced pool more than six hours a day for his role as a hustler in a two-part episode of television's "Dr. Kildare." Peter Falk and James Caan also showed a special talent for pocketing balls on-camera. The late Sir Laurence Olivier stroked a perfectly executed four-rail bank shot in the movie *Sleuth*.

Naturally, *The Hustler* set the standard for pocket billiards in the movies. The 1960 film, featuring Jackie Gleason and Paul Newman (both better-than-average pool players), depicted the seamier side of the game. It also included the best billiard footage ever to grace the big screen.

The Hustler was based on a novel by the late Walter Tevis. Tevis's novel, however, was spawned from a 1958 short story he had submitted to *Playboy*. This is significant, according to pool author and media whiz George Fels, because the old "Philco TV Theater" aired an episode called "Goodbye, Johnny" (well before *The Hustler*'s release), which resembled the *Playboy* short story. "Goodbye, Johnny" starred Cliff Robertson, making Robertson (*not* Newman) the original "Fast Eddie" Felson. (A trivia buff's trivia question!)

While most pool enthusiasts will quickly call to mind *The Hustler* and the more recent *The Color of Money* (marketed in Japan as *The Hustler II*), few remember a box-office dud from the late seventies called *The Baltimore Bullet*. A $4.5 million disaster, the film starred James Coburn, Omar Sharif, and Bruce Boxleitner as traveling con artists and included the top 10 players in the country in cameo roles. After spending weeks filming one pool scene after the next and staging a tournament for the pros, however, the producers edited most of the pool scenes right out of the movie.

The Three Stooges bump cues instead of heads in "I'll Never Heil Again."
(courtesy of The Billiard Archive)

Milton Berle was a decent player in his day, as billiard contenders Allen Hall (left) and
Jay Bozeman (right) could attest. (courtesy of Brunswick Corp.)

What the billiard industry had hoped would be *Son of the Hustler* turned out to be one of the year's biggest flops!

It took Newman's return as "Fast Eddie" to assure another silver screen–driven billiard revival, which is exactly what the 1986 film *The Color of Money* managed to do. Newman, who finally captured an Oscar for his role, and sidekick Tom Cruise dazzled theatergoers around the world. The movie is generally credited with launching billiards to its current status as *the* sport of the nineties.

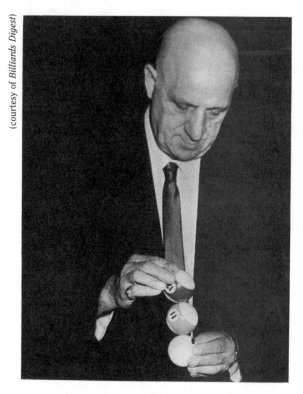
(courtesy of Billiards Digest)

It doesn't take much imagination to figure out how the late Carl Zingale, a terrific exhibition player, earned the nickname "Cue Ball Kelly."

One of the truly endearing traits of these road warriors is the monikers by which they are known. Few players, especially those from the sixties, traveled without a calling-card nickname.

It's funny. There's an old saying: "A good name will wear out; a bad one may be turned; a nickname lasts forever." Is that ever the truth. I can't count how many players I've known by nickname only. If I had to look a player up in the local phone book, most of the time I wouldn't have a clue as to where to begin. But if I pulled up to the local pool-room and asked if "Omaha John" is still in town, chances would be good that I'd find him. Word gets around pretty fast!

I remember a couple of old-timers whose playing days were in the past by the time I met them. (Old-time pool players never die, they become referees.) The late Carl Zingale of Rahway, New Jersey, refereed championship

matches well into his eighties. But few people knew him as Carl Zingale. He was the venerable "Cue Ball Kelly." He was even listed in the local phone book as "C. B. Kelly." The reason they called him "Cue Ball" was obvious. The man's head was as smooth and shiny as the balls he racked. Kelly was a colorful man who told stories of pool games against the likes of Al Capone and Dutch Schultz.

Another player-turned-referee was a kindly old California hustler named Maurice "Tugboat" Whaley. "Tugboat" used to referee matches in Johnston City, but he acquired his nickname by dressing in an old coat and captain's cap and pawning himself off as a retired tugboat skipper. He'd strike up a friendly conversation and eventually work his way into a few games of pool. He plied his trade at bars and poolrooms along the West Coast, usually in port cities.

Hustlers often wear disguises, either to conceal their true identity or to create the illusion that they're harmless hicks. Auto mechanic overalls present a good picture, as does fisherman attire. For my old friend Jay Helfert, however, all that was needed was a "rug"; hence the name "Toupee Jay." Jay, a player-turned-promoter, used to tell tales of wearing his toupee while playing for money in a particular city, then returning to the same city less than a year later without the toupee and beating the same guys!

There was another player of Johnston City vintage (his name escapes me) who went by the name "Castro." He always came to the poolroom in army fatigues, smoking a huge cigar. (Away from the poolroom he was probably a stockbroker!)

A legendary hustler who still lives and plays in Detroit goes by the name "Cornbread Red." His real name is Billy Joe Burge. He gained the name "Cornbread Red" because he's a Kentucky native, with the Southern drawl to prove it, and his hair used to be apple red. I stress used to be. Today, his hair

(courtesy of *Billiards Digest*)

Bill "Weenie Beenie" Staton, here presenting me with a ring for winning a tournament in his poolroom in the early seventies, earned his living by selling hot dogs.

and trademark Fu Manchu mustache are white. Even "Cornbread's" wife, Bernette, has a nickname. People call her "Shortbread."

"Weenie Beenie" is one of the most unusual monikers ever pinned on a player. The man's real name is Bill Staton, and the nickname came from a chain of hot dog stands he owned in the sixties and seventies. "Beenie" still plays occasionally, although he's semi-retired in Myrtle Beach, South Carolina. (Those must have been good hot dogs!)

One of the greatest players of all time, the late Luther Lassiter, was better known around the country as "Wimpy." A poolroom janitor in Lassiter's home town of Elizabeth City, North Carolina, dubbed him "Wimpy" for the endless number of hot dogs and sodas he could pack away as a teenager.

"Machine Gun" Lou Butera, one of the game's most exciting players, earned his

(photo by Billie Billing)

"Machine Gun" Lou Butera is one of the most ▶ colorful players the game has ever known. Crowds love his rapid-fire style.

(courtesy of *Billiards Digest*)

Back in the sixties, Danny Jones was known as "Handsome Danny." The years have taken their toll, however, and Jones is now known as "Dirty Danny."

match in the early seventies. It seems every time Sigel missed a shot, he left his opponent with no clear shot at the lowest-numbered object ball. In pool jargon, his opponent was "hooked." After several such occurrences, Sigel's frustrated opponent threw up his hands, saying, "Who are you? Captain Hook?" The name stuck.

Some nicknames are borrowed, as was Hubert Cokes's title, "Daddy Warbucks." Cokes was another product of the Johnston City tournaments. He was always immaculately dressed in a sharp business suit and smoked a big cigar. A close friend and traveling companion of the most notorious hustler of all time, "Titanic Thompson," Cokes was well-spoken and a favorite of the writers who

"handle" for the rapid-fire style with which he pocketed balls. How quickly does "Machine Gun" pull the trigger? At the 1973 World Invitational, Butera ran 150-and-out against Allen Hopkins in all of 21 minutes! (And "Cue Ball Kelly," who refereed the match, went to his grave swearing Butera actually accomplished the feat in 18½ minutes.)

Some players have been forced to change their nicknames over the years. In the late sixties, a Johnston City perennial named Danny Jones was known as "Handsome Danny." Well, the years have taken their toll, and Danny isn't so handsome anymore! His reputation for utilizing questionable tactics to gain an edge on his opponents led to his current moniker, "Dirty Danny."

Most of the nicknames used by contemporary players are forced and contrived. But Mike Sigel's nickname, "Captain Hook," came about while he was playing a Nine-Ball

(courtesy of *Billiards Digest*)

Evansville, Indiana oilman and high roller Hubert Cokes was known to all as "Daddy Warbucks."

besieged Johnston City whenever the hustlers rode into town.

Some other nicknames I always found amusing were "New York Blackie" (Al Bonife of Brooklyn, a dark-complected man with jet black hair), "The Knoxville Bear" (the great Eddie Taylor, a rather large Tennessean), "Cowboy Weston" (Charles Weston, a world champion from the early 1900s who occasionally dressed in full cowboy gear), and "Tuscaloosa Squirrel" (Alabama's Marshall Carpenter, a scrawny little fellow).

Perhaps the most famous nickname of all, however, belongs to the ageless Rudolph Wanderone. Wanderone, who liked to call himself "Triple-Smart," is far better known as "Minnesota Fats." How did the fat man from New York, who later lived in southern Illinois, come to be known as "Minnesota Fats"? That's a story in and of itself.

Charles "Cowboy" Weston lassoed the world pocket billiard title in 1909.

⚞ FATS OR FICTION? ⚟

Ask a billiard aficionado to list the best players of all time. Without hesitation, the names would burst forth: Hoppe, Mosconi, Greenleaf, Schaefer, Crane, Taberski, De Oro, Cochran.

Ask the exact same question of the average man on the street, and the answer is most likely to be "Minnesota Fats." Hands down, the most recognizable name in pool belongs to 89-year-old Rudolph Walter Wanderone, Jr., of New York City.

Or does it?

In the forties and fifties, Wanderone was a heavyweight gambler, running with the likes of legendary "Titanic Thompson" and Hubert "Daddy Warbucks" Cokes. Wanderone, then known as "New York Fats," "Double-Smart Fats," and "Brooklyn Fats," was a streetwise card shark, pool hustler, and master of the proposition.

Then came *The Hustler*. Based on a novel by an Ohio University professor named Walter Tevis, *The Hustler* starred Paul Newman as "Fast Eddie" Felson, and Jackie Gleason as a portly hustler named Minnesota Fats. There were natural similarities between Gleason's character and Wanderone—the name "Fats" and the reputation as a high roller among them.

There were also several noticeable differences, the most obvious of which is the movie "Fats's" taciturn nature. Anyone who has ever seen Rudolph Wanderone knows that he is a man of many words, most of them ending with -est (as in "greatest," "richest," "biggest" . . .).

Regardless, Wanderone insisted the novel was based on his life, a claim the late

(courtesy of *Billiards Digest*)

In the mid-sixties, Rudolph Wanderone (left) was truly "The Fat Man." At right is Hubert "Daddy Warbucks" Cokes, one of Wanderone's traveling companions.   (courtesy of *Billiards Digest*)

The bluster and braggadocio of Rudolph "Minnesota Fats" Wanderone "sharked" players before the first ball was even struck.

Tevis refuted. "The characters were all made up," said Tevis in an interview in 1980. "There's some highly disguised autobiography in the character of Eddie, but Minnesota Fats was purely fictional."

The truth doesn't matter much. There is little doubt that Tevis's novel and movie were greatly enhanced in later years by Wanderone's adoption of the moniker. As "Minnesota Fats," Wanderone's role as comic, orator, and publicity generator has had an enormous impact on the game in terms of exposure. And Tevis's splendid novel paved the way for Wanderone's future.

The real winner of the Tevis/Wanderone tussle, of course, has been pool. In the immortal words of Wanderone himself, "Pool's the greatest game on earth. You can put two eight-year-old kids on a pool table and go to Europe for a week. When you come home, those two kids will still be at the table, playin' pool!"

HOW TO CREATE YOUR OWN NICKNAME

Once you've honed your playing skills, purchased your first custom two-piece cue, and have a decent handle on poolroom parlance, you may want to consider a nickname. Nothing ostentatious, mind you. Just a little tag to add a romantic twist to your new life-on-the-edge avocation.

To be honest, I've never really had a nickname that stayed with me. For a while, when I was still teaching grammar school, some players called me "Teacher." Now, I'm usually referred to as "Miz."

If you'd like to establish a playing handle, creating a nickname is really fairly easy.

There are certain categories from which to choose. Just find the combination that sounds the most natural. A little name-dropping at the local poolroom, and pretty soon you've got a reputation!

Let's start with your physique. Are you tall? Short? Fat? Skinny? Do you have unusually large feet? (Although I believe "Big Foot" is already taken.) Any facial hair?

How about your city and state?

Simply combine the elements from the two categories which describe you, and you're on your way. Or pick one element and attach it to your first name.

I've known plenty of players whose

(photo by Billie Billing)

Mike Sigel's uncanny propensity for leaving his opponent in an unenviable position accounts for his nickname, "Captain Hook."

(photo by Billie Billing)

Simple, yet perfect. Few nicknames fit a player as well as "Boston Shorty" fits Larry Johnson.

names were spawned from that simple system. There's "Minnesota Fats," "Hawaiian Brian" Hashimoto, Larry "Boston Shorty" Johnson, "Connecticut Johnny" Vevis, "Freddy the Beard" Bentivegna, and "Buffalo Danny" DiLiberto, to name a few. Just like that, you could become "Rhode Island Slim," "Mustache Pete," or "Chicago Heights Phil."

Not interested in the physical attribute/ geographic motif? Don't worry. How about your ethnic background? Does "Frank the Greek" or "Irish Dan" work for you?

Speaking of work, using your profession as part of your nickname makes a statement. It tells people you take your work and play very seriously. I know a cue maker in New York who used to be with the N.Y.P.D. He's still known as "Pete 'da Cop." Then there was old "Doc" Hazzard, whose father owned a hospital, and Joe "the Meatman" Balsis, whose family still runs a meat-packing business. The "profession" approach may better suit your style. Virtually every town has a

"Pete the Barber," but can he cut object balls as well as nose hairs?

Unfortunately, some professions don't lend themselves to nicknames too well. How intimidated is your opponent going to be when you tell him or her that you're known as "Ellen the Social Worker"? Accountants may also have a problem, although "Joey Numbers" actually has a nice ring to it.

A personal style or flair can help create a good nickname. Are you a methodical player? How about "Slow Moe"? There's a money player from Detroit named Edgar White who has a great big pearly-white smile and style all his own. They call him "Shake 'n' Bake."

If you're still having a difficult time choosing a name that fits, don't despair. Do you have any hobbies other than pool? (Sorry, gardeners, but "Tony Green Thumbs" just won't cut it.)

Finally, if you can't come up with a suitable name, just tell your opponent you're "Mike Mosconi, nephew of Willie."

4
Pool Terms

I have to give the inventors of billiard games credit; when they developed the various cue games, they defined the elements with terminology that would last. Aside from colloquialisms and regional slang, pocket billiard terms have changed very little in the past 50 years. Most terms have very literal meanings, such as "carom," "pockets," "foul," and "frozen."

Some terms, however, like "scratch," have changed slightly in meaning over the years. Then there are instances in which terms have been Americanized. The English refer to sidespin on the cue ball as *screw*, a term you're not likely to hear in an American poolroom unless, of course, a player is venting his frustrations! The American billiard term *follow*, referring to spin on the cue ball that causes it to roll forward after contact with an object ball, is more than 140 years old. In the early 1800s, however, that action on the cue ball was referred to as *walking*, or *carry-through*.

As early as 1775, billiard experts were warning unsuspecting enthusiasts of the dangerous "sharps" who lurked in the game's playing establishments. Naturally, this reference was to "hustlers" preying on innocent victims. The exact phraseology of this warning (from a book called *The Annals of Gaming*) is so precise and eloquent, it bears repeating: "In proportion as they advance the

betts [sic], the sharper will lug out his play, and the stranger will be astonished to find, at his cost, the worst player in the world at first, in the end turns out to be one of the best."

I wish I had read that book in my younger, more naive days!

For the most part, billiard terminology is literal. A rail is "a horizontal bar which serves to enclose" the playing area. A cushion is certainly "a padded surface."

But not all billiard terms came into existence so naturally. In fact, the roots of several expressions show that the meanings of the terms have changed somewhat over the course of time.

POOL

Perhaps the most frequently debated term in the billiard dictionary, *pool*'s origins have been traced to the early 1800s and the French word *poule*, meaning a collective stake or ante. The collective bet in multi-player games, such as "Life Pool," a popular English billiard game established around 1819, led to forms of the game being referred to as pool. The term's connection with gambling may have stemmed from the fact that betting parlors of the day, called "Pool Parlors" after the pooling of bets, frequently installed billiard tables to keep their customers entertained.

BILLIARD TERMS. ILLUSTRATED. *"A Kiss!"*

(courtesy of The Billiard Archive)

❦ BANNING "POOL" ❧

The billiard industry still cringes whenever it hears the word *pool* mentioned. Even today, newspaper articles and television spots citing the industry's attempts to rid the game of its "bad image" refer to the insistence on using the term *pocket billiards*.

This war of phraseology is not new.

The use of the term *pool* has been in existence since 1800, probably earlier. That the term took on a negative connotation has dogged the industry since. In fact, in 1921, the Brunswick-Balke-Collender Co. waged a campaign to strike the term *pool* completely. *Pocket billiards* was the only term to be used. "Pool," said Brunswick, "is ambiguous, meaningless, and obnoxious."

The campaign made inroads—briefly. In 1922, a law was passed in New York banning the terms *pool* and *pool parlor* from public view. Only the terms *billiards* and *pocket billiards* were allowed on signs. The law also prohibited persons under 18 from entering a *billiard parlor*.

A COMBINATION SHOT

COPYRIGHT, 1907. BY ROSE HYMAN.

(courtesy of The Billiard Archive)

ENGLISH

Referring to the spin applied to the cue ball by striking it to the right or left of center, the exact origin of *English* is not known. The term was used in a billiards context as early as 1873. The strongest explanation is that English players visiting the United States in the mid-1800s demonstrated various spins applied to the cue ball. Their American counterparts may well have henceforth referred to this new phenomenon as *English*. In fact, the English refer to this action on the cue ball as "screw."

CUE

The word *cue* is derived from the French *queue*, meaning tail. Before the cue stick as we know it today was designed, billiard games were played with a mace. A mace was a curved wooden malletlike instrument with a wooden head and flat face, attached to a thin wooden handle. The configuration allowed the mace to slide along the cloth and strike a billiard ball. The bulkiness of the mace's head, however, made shots near the rail very difficult. To alleviate the inconvenience, players simply turned the mace around and used the tip of the "queue" ("tail") to complete the shot. Expert players soon found that the queue afforded them greater control over the balls and allowed them to impart spin onto the ball. The cue as a separate device was introduced around 1680.

(courtesy of The Billiard Archive)

A French engraving from the early 1700s depicts the use of the "mace." As players became proficient in using the tip of the "queue," or tail-end of the mace, the cue as we know it today came into being.

(courtesy of The Billiard Archive)

The term *scratch*, referring to pocketing the cue ball, derived its name from the infraction's penalty. The opposing player "scratched" a point off the shooter's score, which was normally kept on a chalkboard. In this case, the loser can't even scratch up enough money to pay off his lost wager!

SCRATCH

Strictly an American term, initially it was a colloquialism used by followers of the sport in the mid-1800s to describe a lucky shot. By the early 1900s, a *scratch* became synonymous with a player pocketing the cue ball or fouling in a manner that usually resulted in the deduction of a point (or a number of points) from the shooter's score. Because scoring was kept by making a series of marks on a chalkboard, a scratch literally meant the scratching of a point from the shooter's tally on the chalkboard.

GETTING THE LINGO DOWN

Every sport has its own lingo, a myriad of idiomatic expressions that serves to reinforce the collective spirit—often, though not necessarily, to the exclusion of outsiders. The pool subculture, to those who know it, is obviously no exception. The lingo used by its denizens has lent color and character over the years and is as unaffected by changing times as it is by geographical divide. For the as-yet uninitiated, here's a much-abridged prosaic glossary of common pool slang.

A *player* (the highest accolade in pooldom) will usually wind up with *the nuts* (an enviable situation) or a *lock* (a can't-lose proposition) when he finds *action* (a gambling outlet). That's because he plays *strong* (ruthlessly) for the *cheese* (money). He's got *heart* (courage), and he's not afraid to *high-roll* (play for large sums), especially if he's got a *backer* or a *stake horse* (financial sponsor).

A player, when he's in *dead stroke* (playing his best), has little time for *nits* (nickel-and-dime gamblers), *shortstops* (local champions), *locksmiths* (players who will haggle forever to get an edge), or *cripples* (can't play at all), although any of the above might be a prospective *fish* (an unrealizing, thoroughly outclassed opponent) who could *go off* (lose one's senses and one's money—which can even happen to a player) at any time. For a player to make a game, he often has to give *weight* (a handicap), which, if he's not careful, can turn into *wood* (as in "too much wood to chop"). In such a case, he may have to turn to *sharking* (disturbing one's opponent through distractions or psychological ploys).

Pool players may sometimes resort to *hustling* (deceiving one's opponent for eventual gain) by *stalling* (deliberately missing or misplaying position) or *lemonading* (winning in a seemingly lucky manner or deliberately losing). When a player does this, he keeps from showing his *speed* (true ability). Disreputable pool players have been known to engage in *business*, *dumping*, or *tanking* (losing on purpose) in order to share monies that have been wagered *on the side* (between persons other than the two players). In such a situation, the match is *wet*, or *in the tank* (you could get splashed).

The *sweator* (pool spectator) is often a side bettor. His terminology for the amount he wagers may seem confusing to the layman. Generally speaking, a *fin* or *pound* is $5; a *sawbuck*, $10; a *double saw*, $20; a *yard* or *dollar*, $100; *two dollars* or a *deuce*, $200; a *nickel*, $500; a *dime*, $1,000; and a *big nickel*, $5,000. If sweators are *rolling* (betting high), they may ask to *put it up* (have a third party hold the wager), especially when dealing with a *nit* or a *bust-out* (person who rarely has money).

To *fade* and to *dog* are two of pool's more current colloquialisms. The former means to cope with or to accept, as in, "I can't *fade* that action" or "I can't *fade* the service in the restaurant." To *dog* means to miss in the clutch, or simply the inability to perform up to one's speed, as in, "He's doggin' it." Regarding the use of this term, Danny DiLiberto, a true player, who also bred canines, once had this to say: "Why does everybody have to use that word [dog]? It's unfair; it's a negative term. You're talking about man's best friend."

Letting sleeping dogs lie, I submit a few miscellaneous barks from some former players:

"Don't give me that *Who-shot-John* [phony innocent act]!"

—*Minnesota Fats*

"He's a no-good bum, a *businessman* [prone to *dumping*]."

—*Cue Ball Kelly*

"I believe I've got *the Brazilians* [an exotic form of *the nuts*]."

—*U. J. Puckett*

"Stay away from that guy; he's a *goalie* [a person who won't ever score and doesn't want anyone else to, either]."

—*Little Dog*

It's ironic that the two most well-known, pool-related expressions in the outside world are totally disdained by the cognoscenti. "Dirty pool" is completely irrelevant, for aside from out-and-out cheating, what's dirty? It possibly comes from *pourin' on the oil* (safety play), which to a *cripple* may seem like a form of dishonesty. As for "behind the 8-ball," meaning to be at a disadvantage, well, there are nearly a million ways to get *out-of-line* (improper cue ball position) within a game. Singling out any specific one to signal overall misfortune makes little sense. Besides, it's got a chump's ring to it.

SHAKESPEARE AND "THE NUTS"

As every student of billiards history knows (or should know), one of the English language's earliest references to the green felt can be found in Shakespeare's *Antony and Cleopatra*. Specifically, at the beginning of Act II, Scene V, Cleopatra utters those few words that have befuddled pool academicians for decades: ". . . let's to billiards."

Hold it. Pool in Egypt, roughly 40 B.C.? It's unlikely the great bard was trying to con anybody into thinking that the sport was actually around in those days; rather, this seems to be a case of poetic license. See, the Queen's on tilt from this romance with Antony—and what better way to lighten up than to rack 'em up? Stretching things just a little (maybe a lot, actually), we can find clues as to the dramatist's intent in the greatly overlooked following lines of dialogue between Cleo and her attendants, Charmian and Mardian.

(illustration by Terry Luc)

Was "Fast Cleo" pool's first hustler?

"My arm is sore: best play with Mardian," is Charmian's answer to her mistress's invitation. This is nothing but an outright con. Sure, Charmian—you've got a bum wing, and you can't lift a cue. Right. Maybe the bard originally had you say, "My arm is sore: would'st thou give me weight, madam?" That isn't all. The Queen then says matter-of-factly to Mardian, "As well a woman with an eunuch play'd/As with a woman.— Come, you'll play with me, sir?" That line is the earliest version of "I'll play anybody in the house." And as for her invitation to Mardian the eunuch, it's no less than an order to "Get on up, monkey." His careful answer, "As well as I can, madam," I see as a sly, "I'll try you some, Queenie." Hey! They're all sharking each other!

I submit that the preceding, starting with the famous ". . . let's to billiards," is simply the cornerstone for contemporary pool parlance, whereby a dog is not a man's best friend, the nuts are not a snack, and sweating has little to do with perspiration—depending, of course, on which side you're betting.

If Shakespeare could drop in on a pool tournament or a poolroom today, he might overhear something like this lament from a disgruntled loser: "Really brutal. I got the nuts. I'm on the hill, in dead stroke, and the guy I'm playin' is doggin' it. I get hooked on the break, and he winds up with a road map. Next thing, he turns into King Kong and runs five-and-out. Brutal."

Translating the above for the possibly baffled bard, we'd get something like, "Overwhelmingly depressing. I'm the favorite. I need one game for the match, I'm playing well, and my opponent has a case of the nerves. After my break, I'm left with no shot, and my opponent is left with the balls spread wide open. At this point his play becomes formidable and he wins five consecutive games without missing for the match. Overwhelmingly depressing.

So, the next time you're down at the local poolroom and some shortstop gives you the classic, "Wanna play a little Nine-Ball?" answer him with, "I'll try you some pocket-a-piece (One-Pocket) for a dollar, but we gotta put it up." Now, if he takes you literally and fishes out one dollar to be held in escrow, you've probably got a lock.

If, however, he peels off a couple of C-notes and says, "Let's make it a deuce," you can always quote Cleopatra: "Let's to billiards." Or better yet, quote her sidekick, Charmian: "My arm is sore."

—"Getting the Lingo Down" by John Stravinsky. Reprint by permission of *Billiards Digest.*

(courtesy of *Billiards Digest*)

5
The Fundamentals

Let me start with a very basic premise: nothing is easy for a beginner. Pool is no exception. It is a difficult game to master, especially if you don't put a lot of hard work into mastering the fundamentals. Developing good playing habits from the start is as important in learning to play pool as in learning anything else. Persistence and repetition are the keys. It's not unlike a youth taking music lessons. Although the kid wants to jump headlong into his favorite tunes, he or she is instructed to work on technique and scales, over and over and over. Practicing the basics isn't much fun or very glamorous, but your development as a player will come much more quickly if you've established a solid base—good stance, correct grip, solid bridge, and fluid stroke—from which to work.

No one is "too good" to learn the basics. Even top pros from time to time have to step back and reacquaint themselves with the fundamentals. When a professional pool player falls into a rut, more often than not his problems stem from simple flaws in his mechanics. Before you can correct these flaws, however, you have to be aware of what good fundamentals entail.

Proper technique in pool, like in most sports, is not a perfect science. There is no one right way to stand, or one correct way to hold your cue. In baseball, batting stances and the position of a hitter's hands on the bat vary dramatically. The same holds with golf. But, as in baseball and golf, there are some basic principles that must be adhered to if you want to be successful—like keeping your head down and following through properly.

Follow this section carefully. Some of the points are merely recommendations. Some points—like the aforementioned positioning of the head and follow-through—are absolutes. And, by all means, practice these techniques. Don't be afraid to open the book to this chapter and lay it on a pool table while you grab your cue and work on your stance, stroke, etc. Reading and practicing simultaneously will help you better understand the principles involved.

STANCE

Obviously, stance is very important. You must have the proper balance at the table if you expect the other elements of your mechanics to work smoothly and in unison. Balance and comfort are the keys to stance, and because no two people have the exact same physique, a good stance becomes a matter of personal preference. When you see top professionals, like the ones competing in tournaments on ESPN, you notice that their stances vary dramatically—but with two overriding similarities: balance and comfort.

While you are certainly free to put your own personal stamp on your stance, there are some basic principles that should be considered. First, your feet should be wide enough apart so that if someone nudges you (from virtually any angle), you'll be able to hold your balance. Weight should be fairly evenly distributed from one foot to the other, with some weight resting on your bridge hand. The concept is not entirely different than the three-point stance taken in a football game,

except you don't place too much weight on your front hand. You should be able to lift from your stance freely.

You should, as I said before, be comfortable. If you need to bend your knees a bit to remain comfortable, bend your knees. If you prefer a more rigid stance, straighten your legs.

The position of the feet is very important. Both feet should be pointing in the same direction. Don't stand with one foot pointing forward while the other foot is pointing to the side. Consistency here will also help you achieve proper balance.

Some experts say you should stand between 10 and 12 inches from the table. There are no set rules here, either. Your proximity to

(courtesy of Carmine R. Manicone Photography)

While choosing your stance is primarily a matter of comfort, there are several rules of thumb to consider. If you stand with your feet close together, hold the cue away from your body, and tilt your head at an awkward angle, chances are you're not going to be very successful.

the table will be determined by where the cue ball is situated. Again, what's comfortable for you is most important. Just remember, you shouldn't be cramped when stroking. At the same time, you shouldn't be reaching for shots.

One thing that is important is that you adopt a stance and use that same stance on every shot (excepting those occasions on which you must stretch for a shot). Consistency will become a recurring theme as you develop your work habits. Using the same stance for each shot gives you one less thing to worry about.

A simple way to determine whether or not your stance is solid is to walk up to the table, set your feet, and lean over, planting your bridge hand on the table. You should be able to tell right away whether or not you're balanced and comfortable. Do you have freedom of movement without altering your balance? Does the stance feel natural, or are you stiff and uncomfortable?

The same principles hold true for shots which require some stretching. Whether you have to lay out over the table, or stand on your toes, balance is all-important. If you feel like you're about to slip and/or fall over, get up off the shot and adjust your stance. Test your stance by reaching out a little farther than you need for the shot. If you are still comfortable and balanced, your stance is fine. If not, try another stance or use the mechanical bridge.

(courtesy of Carmine R. Manicone Photography)

With your feet spread slightly apart, your back hand positioned on the wrap (6 to 10 inches from the butt end), and your head directly over the cue (12 to 16 inches), your stance will be balanced and comfortable.

I speak from experience on that subject. Several years ago, at a tournament in Columbia, South Carolina, I reached too far for a shot along the rail in a match against a player named Keith McCready. The score was 10-10, with the first player to reach 11 games being the winner. I got careless, reached too far, and slipped as I was stroking the ball. The object ball hung up in the corner pocket, and I lost the match. Had I reset, or adjusted my stance (or used the mechanical bridge), I would have won the match. Losses like that stay with you a long time.

A good, solid stance also takes into account the positioning of your head as you aim. Again, there is no perfect alignment. Some players stand a bit more erect, with their chin several feet above the shaft of their cue. Others keep their chin so low that the cue actually rubs against it. Nearly all English Snooker players lower their chin right down to the cue—mostly because snooker balls are much smaller than pool balls. Either way, be sure your back arm swings freely and you get a good look at the ball.

One thing to consider when determining how high your head should be over the cue stick is your aim. High or low, your sight line should be directly over, and in line with, the shaft of your cue. Most players feel that the lower you get, the better you see the cue ball in relation to the object ball, and the more accurate your aim. Others feel that getting too low makes it difficult to see the contact point on the object ball and distorts your perspective.

A safe starting point is a compromise. Start with your chin a foot above the shaft. Adjust up or down as you play, and make mental notes. It won't take very long to determine where you feel most comfortable and effective.

I used to stand more erect. Now, however, because contact lenses have allowed me to zero in more precisely on the object ball, I'm tending to get a little lower—maybe 4 inches lower than I used to. It's something I've discovered just in the past year or so, proving that nothing is etched in stone when it comes to stance. Adjust as you see fit.

THE FOX AND THE FLY

It is perhaps the most oft-told story on billiards. The dramatic match of September 1, 1865, between Louis Fox and John Deery in Detroit even reads like an Aesop's fable, but it did, indeed, happen.

Deery, a 23-year-old from Cincinnati, was athletic, handsome, and totally fearless at the table. Fox, shifty-eyed and slightly bald, was said to be a prodigious user of chalk whose antics drove his opponents crazy.

After a period of tense struggle, Fox threatened to close out the $1,000 match with a late surge. As legend has it, a pesky fly landed on Fox's cue ball. Attempts to whisk the fly away proved futile, and the rattled Fox missed his next shot. Deery then ran the points needed to win the match. In reality, Fox's dilemma stemmed from a host of flies. The lighting in those days was usually open flame from gas jets, and it was not uncommon for flies to be drawn to the illuminated flame. The intense flames killed the flies, which then dropped onto the table.

The constant interruptions unnerved Fox, and Deery succeeded in pulling out the victory. So distraught was Fox after losing the match that he sprinted from the hall and plunged himself into the Detroit River. His body was not recovered for nearly a year.

Remember, each player creates his own stance. Pool stances are like batting stances in baseball. There are principles which dictate a good stance for beginners, but at the highest levels of play, stances are very pronounced and different. The key is that proper balance, motion, and rhythm all work in unison to produce power and accuracy at the point of contact.

GRIP

The proper grip is not as obvious as many people believe. There are definitely right and wrong ways to grip your cue. The most common offender of the proper grip is the "choker." He likes to squeeze the cue as tightly as he can. Choking the cue is a capital offense and very disruptive to your stroke. A tight grip creates tension, which in turn prevents you from the smooth, fluid stroke necessary to shoot straight. It also keeps you from being able to use any wrist action on your stroke.

Be loose and relaxed. This is something you need to make yourself aware of throughout a match or game. Sometimes, especially when the contest is not going your way, there is a tendency to tighten up on the cue. Your grip can change from one shot to the next, so be aware. I know that when I feel my grip tightening, I'm pressing at the table. Relax.

All that is needed for the proper grip is your thumb and index and middle fingers. Your ring finger and pinky should be doing nothing more than resting on the butt. There should be no space between the cue and the area between your thumb and index finger. There *should* be a little air between the cue and the palm of your hand. The space between palm and cue should increase slightly on your backswing. On the follow-through, your hand should come down onto the cue— but do not squeeze the cue any tighter.

(courtesy of Carmine R. Manicone Photography)

Notice how the open palm is gripping the cue. All that's needed is your thumb and index and middle fingers. Your other two fingers should do little more than touch the cue.

As for placement of the grip hand, don't get caught up gripping the cue in the exact same spot on each shot. In fact, your grip will change location on almost every shot. A rule of thumb: at the point of contact with the cue ball, your back hand should be perpendicular to the floor. In other words, your elbow should make a nice 90-degree angle at the point of contact.

To find the right gripping spot on any particular shot, try this procedure: after you've made your bridge, take a few practice strokes and stop the cue tip at the edge of the cue ball. Is your back hand pointing directly to the floor? It should be. Without moving the cue, slide your hand forward or back until you find the 90-degree angle. Now take a few more practice strokes before you shoot.

On shots where you are bridging close to the cue ball, your grip will be farther up on the cue. For shots requiring a longer bridge (shots out in the middle of the table, for instance), your grip will be closer to the butt end of the cue.

It should also be mentioned that, regardless of the shot, your bridge hand and grip hand should be the same distance apart. For

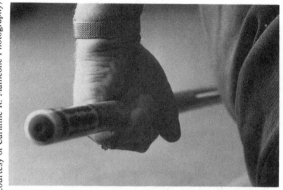

(courtesy of Carmine R. Manicone Photography)

This is the *wrong* way to hold a cue. Don't choke it! The tighter your grip, the less accurate your stroke.

(courtesy of Carmine R. Manicone Photography)

Here's another view, this time from the side, of a grip that is far too tight. Relax. It takes very little strength to stroke a pool cue!

example, if your bridge hand is closer to the tip of your cue, your back hand should also move up. If you are using more shaft, and your bridge hand is back farther on the cue, your grip should be back farther on the butt.

(courtesy of Carmine R. Manicone Photography)

When you're in your stance, position your gripping hand so that your arm is perpendicular to the cue at the point of contact with the cue ball. Your elbow should make a perfect "L" shape.

MAXIMILIAN

Tales of money wagered on billiards are not uncommon, but not many bettors can lay claim to causing the collapse of an entire country! Maximilian II Emanual, the Elector of Bavaria, can.

"Mad Max" was a member of the Wittelsbach dynasty that ruled the tiny Alpine nation for almost 700 years. Max was also addicted to billiards. In fact, while Franco-Bavarian forces waged battle against Europe's Grand Alliance in the War of the Spanish Succession (1701), Maximilian continued to fight his own personal wars on the baize.

Unfortunately, Maximilian will never be known for backing winners. His troops were taking a pounding, as was the royal treasury, which showed $3.6 million unaccounted for. Maximilian later admitted he'd had better days at the gaming table, but he tried to assure his countrymen that his luck would soon change.

Unimpressed, the public demanded he step down. (Maybe the mile-long line of cue-wielding challengers outside the royal palace waiting for a game was the tip-off.)

BRIDGES

Many beginning players are overwhelmed by the variety of bridges used and touted. The key here is to start slowly, testing the simple bridges, then build to the more complex bridges once you gain some knowledge and understanding of what the bridge allows you to do.

There are several basic bridges you can use when your bridge hand is on the table. There are other bridges that come in handy when you're shooting along the rail, and still more bridges available to assist you when you're forced to shoot off of the rail itself. Again, don't try to load yourself down with too many elaborate bridges too quickly. Keep things simple, then add more elements to your arsenal as you become more comfortable.

Five-Finger Open Bridge: The most rudimentary bridge, which all beginners should learn, is the five-finger open bridge. It's simple, solid, and more than adequate for shots that don't require spin or a long reach. Don't dismiss this bridge as "child's play."

To make the open bridge, simply make a fist and place your hand on the table. The heel of your hand should be firmly on the table, with the back of your hand facing up. Now bring your thumb up to the side, forming a "V" between the thumb and the first knuckle. Rest the shaft of the cue in the "V" and slide it back and forth. It's that easy.

Flat Open Bridge: An extension of the five-finger open bridge is the flat open bridge. From the bridge I've just described, just extend your fingers. Keep the heel of your hand on the table, and retain that "V" between your thumb and knuckle. With this bridge, your cue is low enough to impart draw on the cue ball. Your weight is on the tips of your fingers and the heel of your hand. A very easy bridge to learn, yet effective for most shots. For increased stability, spread your fingers apart just a bit.

Forming the open bridge is basically a three-step process. First, make a fist and plant your hand flush on the table.

Leave your hand in place and simply bring your thumb up to form a groove.

To shoot, just glide the cue over the "V" groove between your thumb and fingers.

To form the open flat bridge, start with the closed flat bridge and simply extend your fingers.

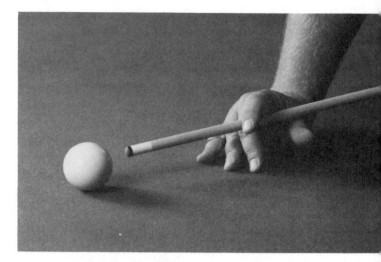

The closed bridge provides the most stability and allows you to use more speed in your stroke. Begin by bringing your index finger over the top of the shaft and lifting your thumb slightly.

Next, bring the pad of your index finger and your thumb together. Remember to keep the heel of your hand planted firmly on the table. The shaft of the cue should slide freely through the bridge.
(photos courtesy of Carmine R. Manicone Photography)

The drawback to open bridges, naturally, is that you have less control of the cue stick. When you try to impart a little more speed or spin to the cue ball, the cue stick tends to lift into the air. Still, since beginners have little control of any kind at that point, the open bridge is a good stepping stone to bigger things.

Closed Bridge: Once you become comfortable with the open bridge, forming the closed bridge is relatively easy. From the flat open bridge configuration, bring the top of your index finger and the tip of your thumb together to form a loop. Keep your weight on the tips of the other three fingers and the heel of your hand. You may want to spread your three base fingers slightly apart.

The loop your index finger and thumb form around the shaft should be secure, but not so tight that the shaft encounters resistance when sliding back and forth.

The closed bridge is used by all professional players. It allows superior control of the cue, which leads to better control over the cue ball. Any shot that requires something "extra" on the cue ball, be it speed, English, draw, or whatever, is best served by a closed bridge.

Regardless of which bridge you choose, remember that the table is the steadiest piece of furniture in the room. Use it. Your bridge has to have a solid base, or your hand will begin to shake and wobble from the tension. Always rest as much of your bridge hand as possible on the table. That's very important.

When shooting from the rail, try to rest your hand and the cue on the rail, then wrap your index finger over the top of the shaft to serve as a guide. Tuck your thumb under your hand.

To get a better view of the contact point, keep your hand flat on the rail and glide the shaft between your thumb and index finger.

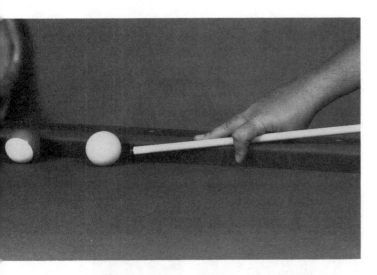

Bridging along the rail is extremely difficult. The idea is to achieve as much control and stability as possible. Using an offshoot of the closed rail bridge, wrap your index finger over the edge of the rail for control.

(photos courtesy of Carmine R. Manicone Photography)

Don't try to shoot in the air!

Rail Bridges: Things get a little more complex when you're forced to shoot along a rail. The easiest rail bridge to learn is the one formed by tucking your thumb beneath your palm and gliding the cue between your index and middle fingers. The tips of your fingers bear most of the weight. Your thumb creates a handy edge along which the cue can slide. This bridge is excellent for shots on which your bridge hand is on the rail. (Never use a closed bridge on the rail!)

For shots along the rail which require you to bridge on the table, rest your index finger along the rail and your other three fingers on the table. Tuck your thumb under your palm, again as a guide, and slide the cue between your index and middle fingers. The cue should be gliding along the edge of the rail.

Another option when shooting along the rail is to form the flat open bridge I explained earlier—but this time rest your thumb on the rail and lift the heel of your hand slightly. This will allow you to form your V groove at rail height.

For shots on which the cue ball is frozen to the rail, the flat open bridge is your best bet. Don't try to use a closed bridge here, because you only have a fraction of the cue ball visible above the rail. Since accuracy is always best when the cue is level, a flat open bridge will give you the best hit on the cue ball.

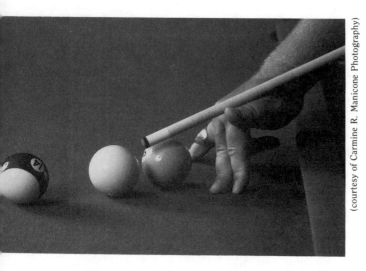

(courtesy of Carmine R. Manicone Photography)

Bridging over an object ball takes a steady hand. The principle here is basically to use the open flat bridge but lift the heel of your hand as high as necessary. All of the balance rests on your fingertips.

Bridging over Balls: When the obstacle to a normal bridge is another ball, the easiest remedy is lifting the heel of your hand as high as needed, while retaining the "V" groove with your thumb. Just be sure to create a firm base with your fingers. Set your bridge hand *before* bringing the cue stick into play to avoid fouling. Place your bridge hand as close to the obstructing ball as possible.

Mechanical Bridge: Some shots are too difficult to reach with any conventional bridge. The best way to attack those situations is by learning to shoot with the opposite hand. However, like gaining ambidexterity at anything, this is very difficult. Few professional players play well enough with either hand to risk shooting opposite-handed in a tournament situation.

Until you become proficient enough to shoot with either hand, those hard-to-reach shots will require the assistance of the mechanical bridge. Practically everyone who has played pool has seen, and probably attempted to use, a mechanical bridge. It's amazing, however, how few people use the "crutch" properly.

The key to using the mechanical bridge is to rest the entire bridge on the table. Don't lift the butt of the bridge off the table. In fact, rest your bridge hand on top of the butt to keep it from moving.

As for your own cue, keep your guiding hand *behind* the cue, not alongside it. The head of the mechanical bridge should be about six inches behind the cue ball (assuming no other balls are obstructing your shot). Also, don't grip your cue with your whole hand. Your thumb and index and middle fingers are all you need. Stand a bit more erect than normal when using the mechanical bridge. Keep the butt end of your cue about chest high, not all the way up by your face. A nice easy stroke is all that's required.

Follow through as you normally would,

(courtesy of Carmine R. Manicone Photography)

Many players are at a loss when it comes to using the mechanical bridge. If you stand upright, hold the bridge up in the air, and aim with the cue at face level, you'll miss the shot and will probably drive your cue tip right into the table!

and be sure that no moving balls run into the mechanical bridge. That would be a foul.

How close to the cue ball should you set your bridge? In most instances, your bridge hand should be approximately 8-10 inches behind the cue ball. More experienced players adjust the length of their bridge. For shots that require minimal movement on the cue ball, they bridge closer to the ball. For shots that require more action on the cue ball, a longer bridge allows for a longer stroke and more action. Beginners should stick with a set distance until they develop a perfectly straight stroke. The farther the bridge is from the cue ball, the more accuracy you sacrifice. This usually doesn't affect professional players, because they've developed such straight strokes.

(courtesy of Carmine R. Manicone Photography)

Properly used, the mechanical bridge can be a game saver. Set the bridge in place, laying it flat on the table. Brace the bridge with your bridge hand, bend slightly at the waist, and direct your sight down the shaft of your cue. (If possible, try to keep the bridge head about a foot away from the cue ball.)

STROKE

Stroking into the cue ball should always be natural and unforced. The key is to get a nice, fluid, back-and-forth motion on the cue. Make sure you have plenty of room for a good backswing and stroke.

Many amateurs and beginning players have a tendency toward a short stroke. They "poke" at the cue ball, pushing it forward. The cue should swing back and forth like a pendulum. The natural motion of your arm swinging forward is all you need to propel the cue ball.

When stroking, don't keep the cue stick too close to your body or too far away from your body. Your back arm should be dangling straight down.

On your backswing, remember to take your stroke as far back as you can without pulling the cue tip completely through your bridge. The proper grip, as we discussed earlier, will allow you to keep the cue straight on your backswing. If you're choking the cue, your wrist will tend to turn, and your stroke is not going to be straight on the follow-through. Let the cue stick do all the work for you. Don't manhandle it.

Always take practice strokes before you shoot. It's a good practice to take the same number of practice strokes on every shot. Again, consistency gives you one less thing to worry about when shooting. When you address the cue ball, set the cue tip near the spot on the cue ball you want to hit. Then take your practice strokes. There is no "perfect" number of practice strokes. One or two may not be enough to lock in your aim. By the same token, it's hard to hold your position and concentration when you take 15 or 20 practice strokes.

Use your practice strokes to make a mental checklist. Is your grip too tight? Is your arm relaxed? Is your stroke fluid? If everything, including your aim, looks and feels okay, fire away!

Without any balls on the table, try some practice strokes by lining your cue up parallel to the rail. Is the cue straight on the follow-through? Peek back at your arm and elbow. Is everything in sync?

Perhaps the most important element in the stroke is the follow-through. The cue tip should follow the cue ball approximately 8 inches. The tip shouldn't go into the air or rip into the cloth. It should go straight *through* the cue ball. And follow through with conviction. Don't use a baby stroke, and don't stroke too hard. Be firm. That's another way to assure a straight stroke.

And don't get caught up thinking that drawing the ball requires a lot more power. You'd be surprised. A nice, easy stroke and a good, smooth follow-through will get plenty of response from the cue ball.

The most important factor in a good follow-through is keeping your head down. The natural tendency is to jump up and admire your handiwork the moment you've stroked the cue ball. Don't fall into that habit! You won't like what you're going to see.

If you ask a top pro to give you one single piece of advice, more often than not he or she is going to say, "Keep your head

(OPPOSITE, UPPER LEFT)
Assume your proper stance and aim to pocket the ball. Notice the "L" shape formed by my back arm? I'm ready to stroke this shot.

(courtesy of Carmine R. Manicone Photography)

(OPPOSITE, LOWER LEFT)
Take a full backswing, bringing the tip of your cue right to the edge of your bridge. Again, don't grip the back end of the cue any tighter than you have to.

(courtesy of Carmine R. Manicone Photography)

(OPPOSITE, UPPER RIGHT)
Follow all the way through the cue ball. Notice that my head is still down, my bridge hand is firm, and I've followed directly through until the tip of my cue is actually touching the cloth.

(courtesy of Carmine R. Manicone Photography)

(OPPOSITE, LOWER RIGHT)
The proper follow-through, as shown from the side. By maintaining a fairly loose grip on the cue, I was able to keep my stroke straight. The butt of the cue isn't raised and, again, my head is still down.

(courtesy of Carmine R. Manicone Photography)

(courtesy of The Billiard Archive)

Robert Cannefax always found a way to make his point, which eventually led to his being cut out of competition.

❦A REAL CUT-UP❧

Three-Cushion billiard champion Robert Cannefax of St. Louis never pretended to be much of a comedian. Nonetheless, the 1920s whiz will always be remembered as a cut-up for his antics in a high-stakes billiard match against Willie Hoppe in Chicago in 1925.

After several blocks of play, the temperamental Cannefax, who preferred a fast cloth, asked for a change. Hoppe, who was leading at the time, said there was nothing wrong with the playing surface and refused to allow a change. An angry Cannefax then drew a pen knife from his jacket and ripped the cloth down the center of the table. Hoppe was awarded the match and Cannefax was suspended from competition for one year.

Incredibly, the Hoppe affair proved to be Cannefax's last match. He spent some time in vaudeville, then died from meningitis in 1928.

My problem on the follow-through here is rather obvious, but not nearly as uncommon as you might think. Many players react to shots in this way without even realizing it. Keep your head *down*, and follow *all the way through!*

down!" Keep your head down all the way through your follow-through. Force yourself. That's especially important at the start, when good and bad habits are most likely to be developed. Exaggerate the technique at the beginning. Stay down a lot longer than needed, just to develop the habit. You'll be a more consistent player in the long run.

Remember, as is the case in most sports, you have to be sure to "finish" properly. A good follow-through and keeping your head down are essential to finishing off a pool shot.

AIMING

Aim is by far the most difficult aspect of the game to learn. Aiming is hand-eye coordination, the transition of thought to action from your head to your arm. Some players never quite get the hang of it. Others make the adjustments in no time at all. In great part, aim is simply a judgment of where to strike the object ball. Consistently good judgment comes with experience (a pro's term for repetition).

Unfortunately, few players can tell you exactly *how* they aim. Most players, even at the highest levels of play, will tell you that aim is a matter of feel. No one is so precise that he can tell you exactly how to aim. But we can help you better understand the concept.

Countless times I've seen an amateur or beginner lay his cue on the table to line up the intended object ball with a pocket. Through this technique, he determines the exact spot the object ball must be hit by the cue ball. That tells him where contact must be made, but is that aiming?

Take the situation in Diagram 1. The dot on the object ball shows where contact must be made to pocket the ball. The problem comes in determining how much of the cue ball should hit that spot. (For all shots in this section, I am assuming a center ball hit—meaning you are striking the center of the cue ball on each shot. Also, it's very important to begin taking aim *before* you lean over to shoot.)

On a straight-in shot, you aim your cue tip to hit the center of the cue ball, sending it to the center of the object ball (Diagram 2). Simple enough. But let's go back to the situation shown in Diagram 1, which requires you to cut at a more severe angle. In Diagram 3, the broken circle represents the cue ball at its contact point on the object ball. Only a small portion of the cue ball will contact the

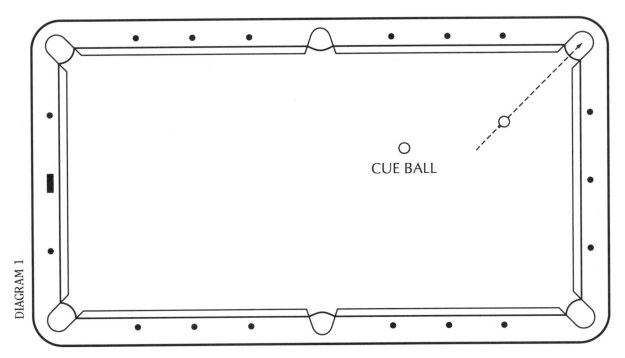

DIAGRAM 1

CUE BALL

The dot on the object ball shows where contact must be made to send the ball to the corner pocket. But what portion of the cue ball must hit that spot?

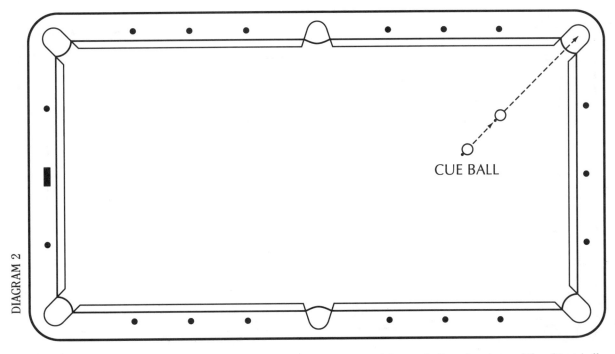

DIAGRAM 2

CUE BALL

For straight-in shots, using a center ball hit, aim to send the center of the cue ball to the center of the object ball. Or aim as though you intended to shoot the cue ball directly into the pocket.

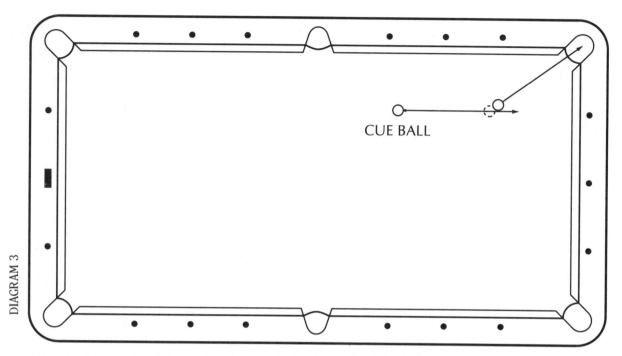

DIAGRAM 3

CUE BALL

If you aimed the center of the cue ball at the contact point on the object ball, you would miss this shot. Only a portion of the cue ball will strike the object ball.

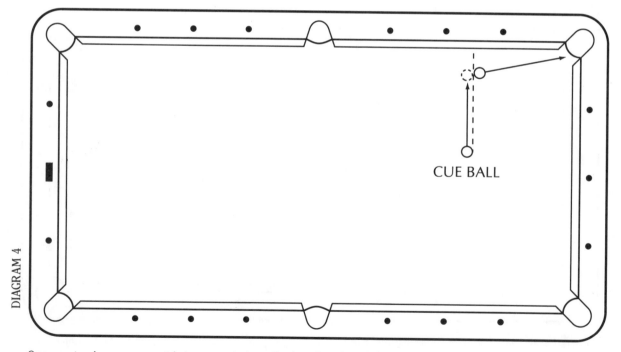

DIAGRAM 4

CUE BALL

One way to aim a severe cut is to concentrate on having the edge of the cue ball touch the edge of the object ball.

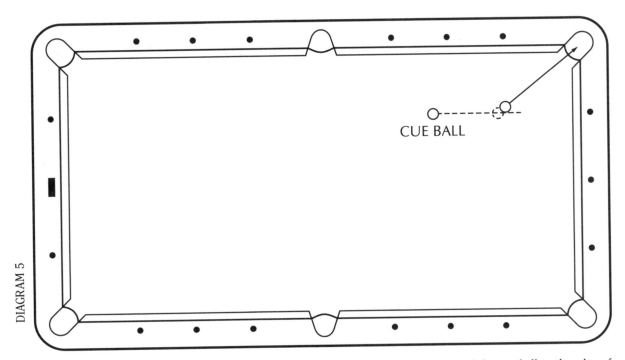

DIAGRAM 5

CUE BALL

On shots requiring a less severe cut on the object ball, try aiming to send the center of the cue ball to the edge of the object ball.

object ball. The point here is that the contact point is not necessarily where you aim the center of the cue ball.

So, then, how do you aim the cue ball on angled shots? Take Diagram 4, which shows that a very thin cut is required on the object ball. One way to aim this shot is to concentrate on having the edge of the cue ball touch the edge of the object ball. Don't concern yourself so much with finding an aiming point for the center of the cue ball. The reason so many beginners make that mistake is because they hit practically all shots with center cue ball. (Center cue ball is fine, but you must make adjustments when aiming.)

On a shot requiring a slightly less severe cut, where approximately half of the cue ball hits the object ball, try aiming the center of the cue ball at the edge of the object ball (Diagram 5).

This may sound intricate, but it's really not. You can develop your own tricks for aim-

ing, but at least this will start you in the right direction.

One of the easiest ways to gauge the way your aim needs to be adjusted is to line up a straight-in shot (Diagram 6). Shoot the same shot over and over. Develop the feel for solid contact. Then move the ball several inches to one side, creating a slight angle. Practice that shot over and over, all the while concentrating on how your aim has changed. Continue moving the cue ball to create a more severe angle. Now move the cue ball to the other side of the straight-in position. Pretty soon you'll have a good idea of how your aim changes to compensate for sharper cuts on the object ball.

CUEING

Once you've developed your aiming skills—that is, you can successfully pocket balls on a better-than-average basis—you'll become in-

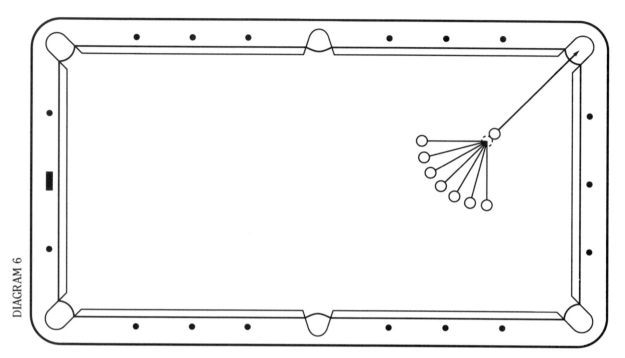

DIAGRAM 6

To learn how much your aim needs to be adjusted on different shots, set the object ball in one spot and move the cue ball to create various angles.

creasingly interested in garnering control of the cue ball. How the cue ball reacts after contact with the object ball is generally determined by where your cue tip strikes the cue ball.

Up to this point, we've concentrated on center ball shots. In theory, if you cue the ball in the center and shoot an object ball straight into a pocket, the cue ball should stop at the point of contact. In reality, it's very difficult to strike the ball with pinpoint accuracy, and nearly impossible to make it stop absolutely in its tracks.

Because you very rarely strike the cue ball exactly in the center, it helps to know how off-center hits affect the cue ball and how you can use off-center hits to your benefit.

For straight-in shots, the cue ball can do just three things: stop, roll forward, or come back toward you. By striking the cue ball above its center, you force the cue ball to *follow* the object ball after contact (Diagram 7). To get the cue ball to come back toward

you, cue the ball below the center, or *draw* the ball. From this point on, I will refer to these actions as simply "follow" and "draw."

Striking the cue ball to the left or right of center imparts side spin on the cue ball, called *English.* All references to English will presume left or right side spin on the cue ball.

STOP SHOTS

Again, don't be concerned if the cue ball doesn't actually stop dead in its tracks. Few players can do that.

By definition, hitting the cue ball in the center on straight-in shots should produce a stop shot. (Remember, a stop shot is only possible on straight-in shots.) However, to get the cue ball to stop it must have no discernable spin on it at the point of contact with the object ball. As you get farther from the object ball, it will become necessary to cue the ball a touch below center to get it to stop on contact. The reason is that after a certain

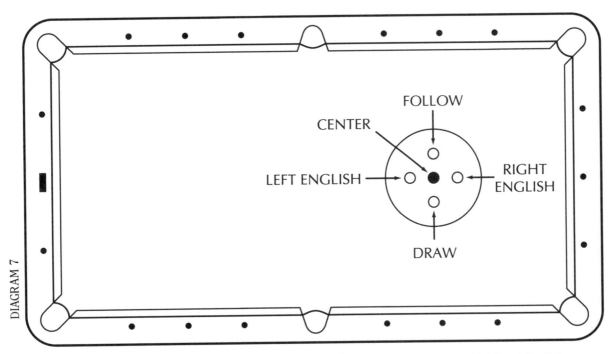

DIAGRAM 7

The five basic ways to cue the ball are center ball, draw, follow, right-hand English, and left-hand English.

distance, the cue ball naturally begins to roll forward.

When the distance between the cue ball and object ball is only a foot or so, using a center ball hit and moderate stroke will cause the cue ball to stop. Beyond that, a little draw is required.

To get an idea of this concept, place the cue ball on the head spot. Remove all object balls from the table. Using a moderate stroke and center hit, watch the rotation of the ball. It will slide without spin for only a short distance, then will begin to roll forward, or follow. Therefore, if you used the same stroke for a shot on an object ball three feet away, the cue ball would not stop on contact. It would follow.

In the same vein, cue the ball below center. It will slide forward, with reverse spin on it, for several feet, then will begin to roll forward. What all this tells you is that to get the cue ball to stop, the cue ball must have no spin on it when it hits the object ball. On a shot four feet away, use a little reverse. By

the time the cue ball reaches the object ball, the reverse spin will have dissipated, and the cue ball will stop in its tracks—or close enough.

FOLLOW

Follow shots are probably the easiest shots to gauge. On a straight-in shot, how far the cue ball follows the object ball is based solely on how high and how hard you strike the cue ball.

Set up a shot aimed straight to the corner pocket (Diagram 8). Cue the ball above center, and use a very delicate stroke. Place a piece of chalk alongside the spot at which the cue ball stopped rolling. Shoot the same shot again, this time using a medium stroke. Again, mark the spot with a cube of chalk. Finally, use a firm stroke and see how close you can come to following the object ball into the corner pocket.

Wouldn't it be nice if all shots were as easily understood as the follow?

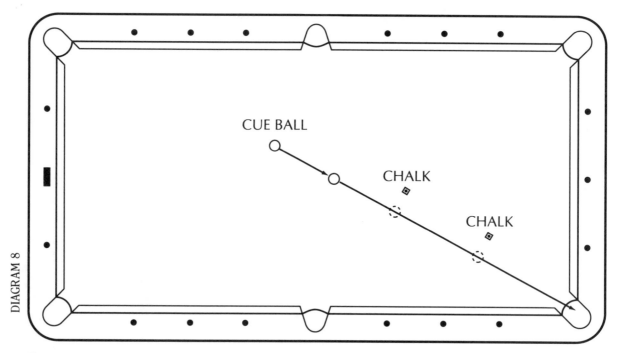

DIAGRAM 8

CUE BALL

CHALK

CHALK

To experiment with follow, shoot a straight-in shot using several speeds. Mark where the cue ball stopped with a cube of chalk, and continue testing different speeds.

DRAW

The first thing to understand about draw is that the cue ball must be struck well below center. To do this accurately and effectively, it is recommended that you lower your bridge hand as much as possible. As mentioned before, the cue should always be level with the contact point on the cue ball. (Obviously, there are instances in which this is impossible, such as trying to draw the cue ball when it is near a rail. On those occasions, you'll need to raise the butt end of your cue, which, on draw shots, restricts your follow-through.)

A common misconception about drawing the cue ball is that you have to hit it harder. Not true. As long as your cue is level and you hit the cue ball below center, a fluid stroke and follow-through is all that's needed on most shots. (Of course, if you need to draw the cue ball the length of the table, more cue speed is necessary.)

ENGLISH

Nearly all top professionals get around the table just fine using only center cue ball, follow, and draw. There are times, however, when English is advantageous.

The reason players try to avoid English is that it imparts side spin on the cue ball. The cue ball reacts differently off the tip, and the object ball reacts differently off the cue ball. Because it's impossible to hit the cue ball to the left or right of center and have it travel in a straight line, you have to adjust your aim to compensate. Simply put, English tends to complicate the shot.

Basically, when using right-hand English, the cue ball will deflect slightly to the left off the cue tip. Left-hand English deflects to the right. Pros usually use English to change the angle from which the cue ball will carom off a cushion. English is also transferred from the cue ball to the object ball

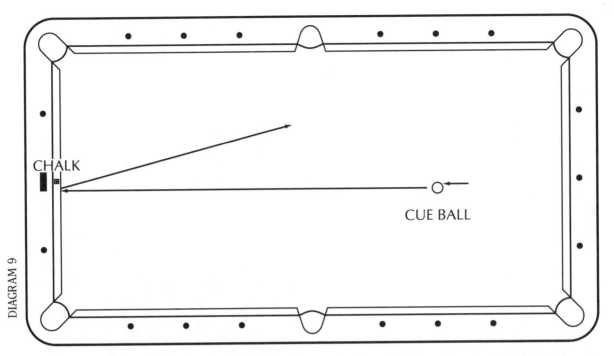

DIAGRAM 9

To understand English, place the cue ball on the head spot and a piece of chalk on the end rail halfway between the corner pockets. Aim the cue ball at the chalk, but strike it with right-hand English. Notice how far the ball deflects to the left, and watch how it reacts off of the cushion.

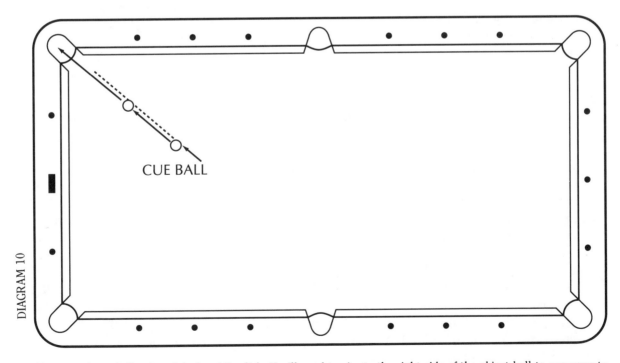

DIAGRAM 10

Try to pocket a ball using right-hand English. You'll need to aim to the right side of the object ball to compensate for the cue ball's deflection to the left.

upon contact, adding yet another complication to the shot.

To better understand the phenomenon of English, place a cue ball on the head spot (Diagram 9). Put a piece of chalk on the end rail, halfway between the corner pockets. Aim the cue ball directly at the chalk, but strike it with right English. Note where the ball actually hits the rail. By striking the cue ball off center, it deflects several inches to the left. Adjust your aim until you can use right English and have the cue ball hit the rail near the chalk.

For practical applications, set up the shot as shown in Diagram 10, and try to pocket the ball using right English. When you come to realize how much your confidence and accuracy dwindles, you'll understand why I'm going to close our discussion of English right here. It's an aspect of the game everyone should know about, but don't attempt to add English to your game until you've absolutely mastered the basics.

French champion Vignaux was a notorious whiner.
(courtesy of The Billiard Archive)

❦ VINTAGE VIGNAUX ❦

Nobody in the billiard world ever accused French champion Maurice Vignaux of being a gracious loser. The hefty Frenchman was well known for throwing whining and pouting tantrums when important matches were not going his way. The first 18.2 Balkline championship, held at the Grand Hotel in Paris in 1903, was no exception.

After six days of play, three of the contestants—Vignaux, countryman Louis Cure, and American George B. Sutton—were tied for first place. A tie-breaking playoff was suggested. Vignaux balked, complaining that such a remedy was irregular. The title, Vignaux rationalized, should be decided based on highest overall average. (Naturally, that alternative favored Vignaux.)

The match was halted—for several months!—while the players took the matter to court. The French court ruled in favor of Vignaux, declaring him the champion based on his high grand average.

POSITION

Up to this point, the main focus has been on pocketing a single ball as if it were the last ball on the table. That's fine for beginners. You should spend as much time as needed refining your mechanics and techniques.

Once you've developed your pocketing skills (that is, you can successfully pocket balls on a better-than-average basis), it's time to move on to the real essence of the game: pocketing as many balls in a row as possible.

There is no greater joy in pool than running a large number of balls in succession. For the beginner, four- and five-ball runs can bring just as much joy as 100-ball runs bring to professionals.

To sink even two balls in a row, you must have a plan of action, a strategy. And the only way to plan an attack is to have control over the cue ball's path *after* it strikes the object ball. Knowledge of the cue ball's path is the crux of position play: moving the cue

ball from object ball to object ball with some preconceived plan of action. Position play is predicated on cue ball control.

I've already recommended that you refrain from using English until your game can handle it, so discussion on position play for beginners will stick to center ball, follow, and draw.

Obviously, for straight-in shots, the cue ball can either stop, follow, or come back toward you. Playing for position after a straight-in shot, then, leaves your options somewhat limited. In Diagram 11, you have a straight-in shot on the 1-ball into the corner pocket. If you use center ball and stop the cue ball, you are left with a relatively long shot at the 2-ball. If you use follow, you're bound to scratch (follow the cue ball directly into the corner pocket) or leave yourself an even longer shot on the 2-ball. By applying draw, you will pull the cue ball back toward the middle of the table, leaving you with an easy shot on the 2-ball. (Through practice, you'll be able to determine just how much draw to

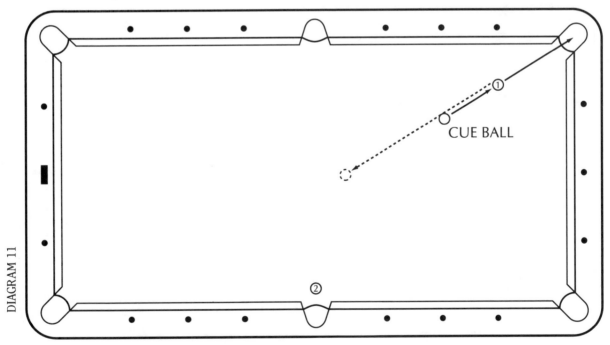

DIAGRAM 11

Because your shot on the 1-ball is straight in, the only way to gain decent position on the 2-ball is to draw the cue ball back to the middle of the table.

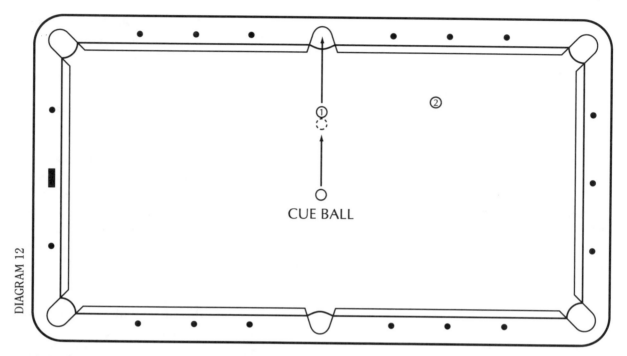

A simple stop shot on the 1-ball will provide perfect position for the 2-ball.

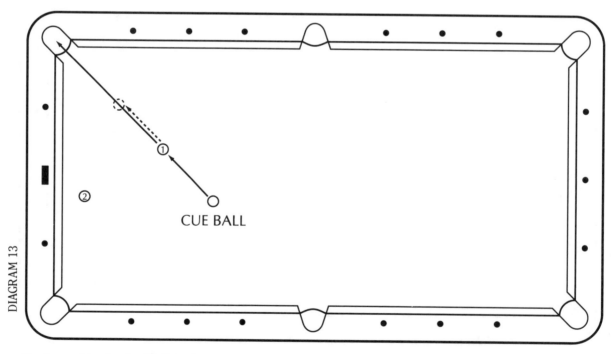

To play position for the 2-ball in this instance, follow the 1-ball with a fairly soft stroke. Remember, don't try to be too perfect. Virtually any spot beyond the original location of the 1-ball will give you a good shot at the 2-ball.

apply. In this instance, medium draw would work out nicely.)

For the straight-in shot in Diagram 12, a center ball stop shot is the perfect solution. Again, following the 1-ball might cause you to scratch and would certainly leave you a difficult angle on the 2-ball. Draw would pull you away from the 2-ball, forcing you to cut the ball. A stop shot will give you a direct line on the 2-ball to the corner pocket.

Following the object ball on straight-in shots almost always presents the greatest risk, because too much follow will result in a scratch. By the same token, follow is easy to apply and is your only choice in some situations. In Diagram 13, using center ball to pocket the 1-ball will leave you almost no shot on the 2-ball. (A right-handed player would have a long reach to cut the 2-ball, and a length-of-the-table bank shot is no cinch.) Drawing the cue ball would leave you with a long, difficult cut to the same corner in which

you pocketed the 1-ball. A little follow is all that's required to give you a simple shot on the 2-ball.

This is very rudimentary position play, but it gives you some idea of how to plot your next shot. Don't be afraid to practice shots like this. Nothing should be deemed "too simple."

Angled shots give you the most flexibility in playing position. To play position off of angled shots, however, you need some idea of how the cue ball deflects off of the object ball and how to adjust that angle of departure.

The easiest place to start is by setting up a fairly easy cut shot. Pocket the ball using center cue ball. When the cue ball strikes the object ball (Diagram 14, broken circle), it will depart along the line which bisects the balls at the contact point (dotted line). Virtually all players, right up to the professional level, work from this principle. Some players refer to this as the Right-Angle Principle, while

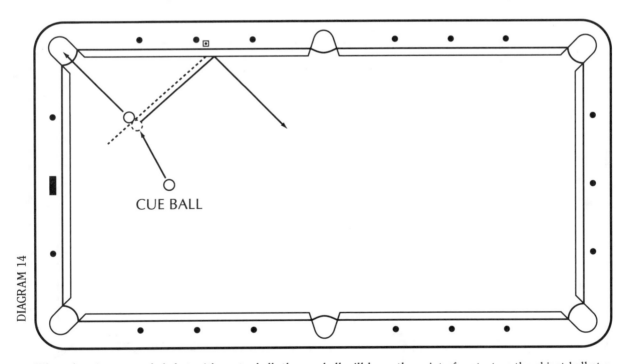

DIAGRAM 14

CUE BALL

When shooting an angled shot with center ball, the cue ball will leave the point of contact on the object ball at a 90-degree angle. Practice this principle by placing a cube of chalk on the rail where the cue ball hit. Then hit the same shot again and again. The cue ball should continue to strike the rail at the same spot.

others call it the 90-Degree Principle. Regardless of what you choose to call it, this is a good base from which to work.

Practice that shot using nothing but a center ball hit. Watch where the cue ball strikes the rail. Assuming you pocketed the object ball, place a cube of chalk on the rail at the spot the cue ball hit. Leave the chalk there and shoot the same shot several more times. As long as you continue to strike the cue ball in the center, it will deflect to the rail directly in front of the chalk every time!

Now, how do follow and draw affect the same shot?

Follow shortens the angle of departure, while draw widens the angle.

This may sound confusing, but it's really very simple. Once you practice and understand this theory, your ability to run several balls in a row will increase dramatically—and that's what makes the game fun.

Set up the same shot as in the previous drill, and leave the piece of chalk in place on the rail. This time, pocket the ball using follow on the cue ball. The cue ball should hit the rail farther down the rail, toward the corner pocket (Diagram 15). Set up and shoot this shot with follow several more times. Keep your eye on where the object ball hits the rail.

Starting to get the idea?

Finally, shoot the same shot using draw—again leaving the chalk in the spot marked by your center ball hit (Diagram 16). Notice how the cue ball slides to a point farther up the rail? Shoot again, keeping an eye on where the cue ball hits the rail.

This exercise is invaluable. It's simple, yet you've just taught yourself one of the most important lessons in pool. This knowledge will help every single phase of your game. It can help you know when you risk scratching into a pocket. It can help you discern how to strike the cue ball to avoid bumping into other balls which might be obstructing its path. Or, if you *want* to bump

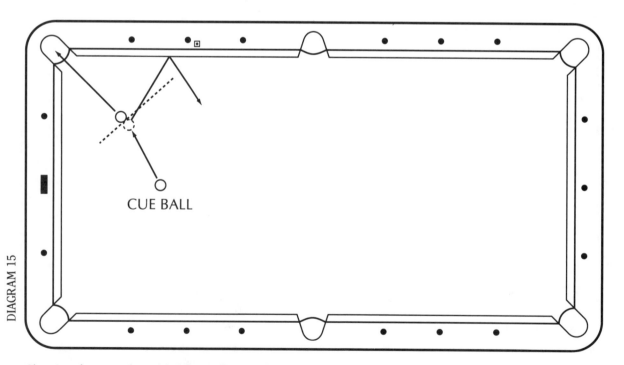

DIAGRAM 15

CUE BALL

Shooting the same shot with follow will cause the cue ball to take a more direct path to the rail.

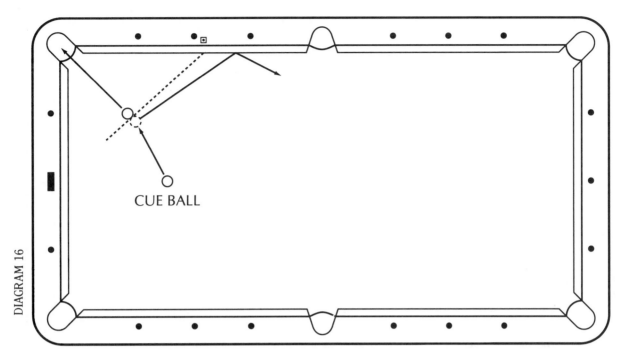

DIAGRAM 16

CUE BALL

Still the same shot with draw will cause the cue ball to slide farther up the table before striking the rail.

into balls to break up clusters, the principle you've just learned will help you figure out how to do that, too.

(One amendment to the above theory you should know. On shots which require a very thin hit—less than half of the object ball—draw and follow have no discernable effect on the cue ball's angle of departure. The cue ball doesn't hit enough of the object ball to react differently. On those shots, draw or follow will only affect the cue ball's reaction off the rail.)

To apply this principle to position play, consider the dilemma posed in Diagram 17. It's the same shot you've been practicing, only now the 2-ball has been added. Based on your newly discovered expertise in cue ball control, you know that draw will slide the cue ball farther up the rail. Plus, the wider angle off the cushion will allow the cue ball to travel up in the direction of the top rail.

In many instances, you can achieve acceptable position using center, follow, or draw. On those occasions, it's up to you to

decide which route is optimum. In Diagram 18 you want to pocket the 1-ball and play position on the 2-ball. While you may be in a position to pocket the 2-ball using any of the three strokes, a center ball hit is your safest bet. By using follow (dotted line A), you risk coming too close to the 2-ball. With draw (dotted line B), you risk scratching into the corner pocket. Center ball will give you a nice cushion.

Amazingly, you've now learned how to move the cue ball to virtually any spot on the table through the use of three simple strokes: center, follow, and draw.

Now, as the commercial says, you can "master the possibilities."

PRACTICE DRILLS

In my second Lite Beer commercial, I close the spot by repeating, "Practice, practice, practice." For the beginning pool player, those are indeed words of wisdom.

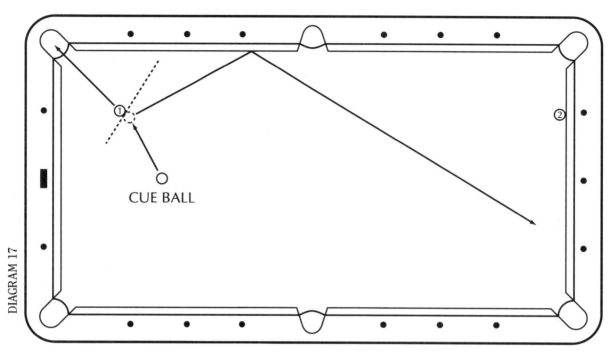

When a second ball is added, use your knowledge of the cue ball's tendencies to determine how to play position. In this case, drawing the cue ball off the 1-ball will bring you into nice position for the 2-ball.

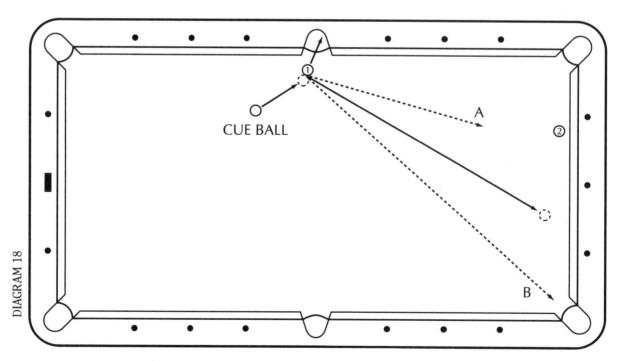

To play position on the 2-ball, think through your options. Follow (A) will bring the cue ball closer to the 2-ball than needed. Draw (B) risks a scratch. A simple center ball hit on the cue ball is a happy medium.

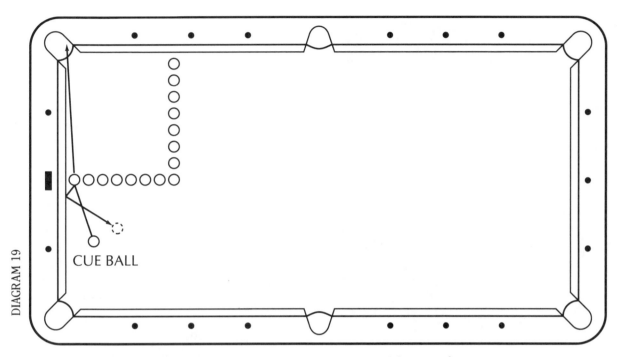

DIAGRAM 19

CUE BALL

Being able to run all 15 balls in succession in the "L" drill requires a delicate touch.

The "L" drill is a fairly standard practice drill. Try to run the balls in sequence, all into the corner pocket. Speed, control, and a delicate touch are necessities here.

(courtesy of Carmine R. Manicone Photography)

Don't fall into the habit of simply throwing balls on the table and trying to shoot them in. For one, it can get extremely boring. Give yourself a set challenge.

There are standard practice drills which have been around for eons but are still great drills. I practiced these drills when I was younger.

THE "L" DRILL

Start with the "L" drill, as shown in Diagram 19. Line up eight balls, a few inches apart, straight out from the middle of the end rail. With the other seven balls, complete the "L" by setting them in a line toward the side cushion.

Place the cue ball near the bottom rail and try to run the balls in order. The common problem beginners run into when practicing the "L" drill is hitting the cue ball too hard and not being in position to shoot the next ball in line. This drill is great for developing a soft touch.

Most importantly, though, you have to

The dreaded "Circle." This drill reinforces your draw and follow techniques. The cue ball must not touch a rail. You may pocket the balls into any pocket.

(courtesy of Carmine R. Manicone Photography)

make sure you pocket the intended object ball. If you miss, you're finished and have to start all over again.

THE CIRCLE DRILL

On the circle drill, use all 15 balls to make a circle in the middle of the table. Leave several inches between balls. Start with the cue ball in the middle and try to run all the balls without allowing the cue ball to touch a rail. Also, don't let the cue ball bump any of the other object balls.

Remember, you don't have to keep the cue ball within the circle, and you don't have to shoot the balls in order. Shot selection becomes very important here. Stop shots, a little follow, and a little draw are all you can use here.

RUN-OUT

This is a great little drill which forces you to think ahead. Throw two balls out onto the table. Take the cue ball in hand, place it anywhere you want on the table, and run the

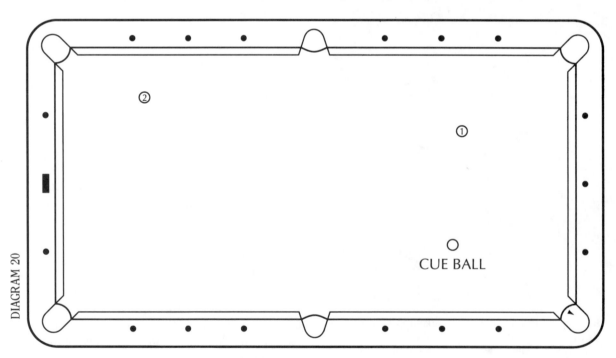

To learn to think at the table, take cue ball in hand and try running these two balls. When that becomes too easy, add a third ball, then a fourth, and so on.

two balls (see Diagram 20).

It sounds easy, but it's a great challenge because it forces you to take a long, hard look at the situation and plot a strategy. Continue to practice this until you find that you can run those two balls no matter where they are.

Once you've mastered that, add a third ball to the drill and run all three. This is where your knowledge of where the cue ball travels will come into play.

Don't try to be too perfect when practicing this drill. Give yourself general areas to aim for. No player can send the cue ball to an exact location time and time again. Just try to reach an area which gives you a good shot on the next ball.

SPECIAL SHOTS

BANK SHOTS

Beginners can get very confused trying to figure out bank shots. Table-side experts will try to teach you intricate banking systems, like "bisect the incoming and outgoing angles to determine the point on the rail the object ball should contact" or "continue your line of aim beyond the rail to an imaginary second table . . . ." You can go crazy trying to memorize and utilize such instructions. Unless you plan on bringing a pad of paper and calculator to the table—which is certain to make you popular with your opponents— keep things simple.

As a rule, the only banks I like are the ones with automatic tellers and vaults.

If you must shoot banks, consider a few basic recommendations. Stay away from any bank shot that requires you to cut the object ball. Until you reach the advanced stage, limit yourself to banks that lay on, or very near, a natural angle. A "natural" presumes a center ball, medium speed, straight-on hit on the object ball. When you strike an object ball in such a manner, it will come off the rail at the same angle it approached the rail (Dia-

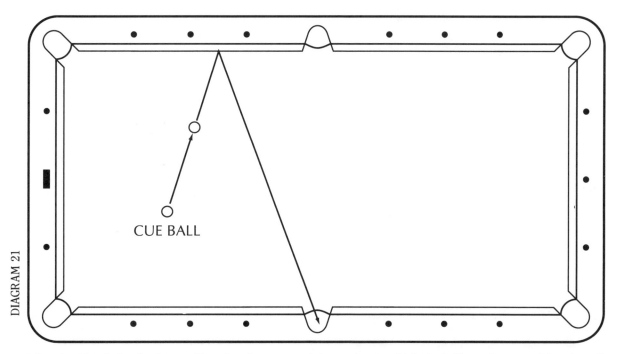

CUE BALL

DIAGRAM 21

When banking balls, the "natural" angle refers to a straight-on shot in which the ball's angle approaching the rail is roughly the same as its angle departing the rail.

gram 21). If that flush hit and natural angle will send the object ball to a pocket, it's worth attempting.

For some reason, most beginners tend to hit bank shots way too hard. I think the mind-set of the amateur player is that, because you're doing something extra to the ball, you need to fire the ball as hard as possible. Not so. Use your normal stroke for bank shots that lie on a natural angle.

If the natural angle looks as though the object ball will hit a few inches short (Diagram 22, solid line) or a few inches beyond the pocket (Diagram 23, solid line), you can compensate by hitting the cue ball harder or softer. A softer hit will cause the object ball to bank a tad longer (Diagram 22, dotted line). If hit more firmly, the object ball will tend to bank a touch shorter (Diagram 23, dotted line).

For now, that is essentially all you should concern yourself with when shooting bank shots. Don't try to impart English on a

bank, and don't attempt to cut the ball. Stick to banks that can be hit straight on and with center ball. If the path needs to be adjusted slightly, do so by hitting the shot harder or softer.

KISSES AND COMBINATIONS

Kiss shots and combinations are also shots which you should avoid for the time being unless they are perfectly "on," meaning they're virtually impossible to miss.

To at least give you an understanding of what kisses entail, refer to Diagrams 24 and 25.

Kiss shots are easiest to gauge if the object balls are frozen. In your mind's eye, draw two lines: one through the centers of the object balls (dotted line A) and another between the balls (dotted line B). If line B cuts directly through line A and into a pocket, the shot is "on." As long as the cue ball strikes the 1-ball (Diagram 24) somewhere in the 90-degree quadrant above the 1-

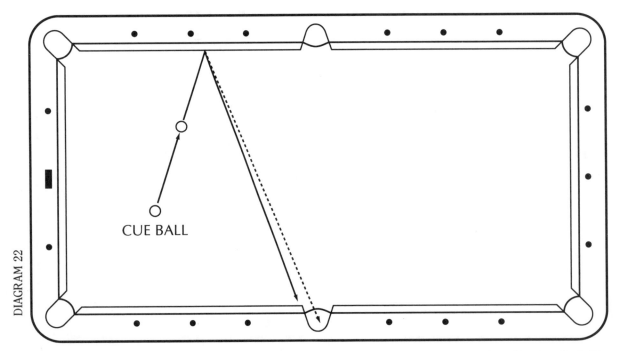

CUE BALL

DIAGRAM 22

If the natural angle of a bank shot leaves the object ball just short of a pocket, a softer stroke will widen the ball's departure angle.

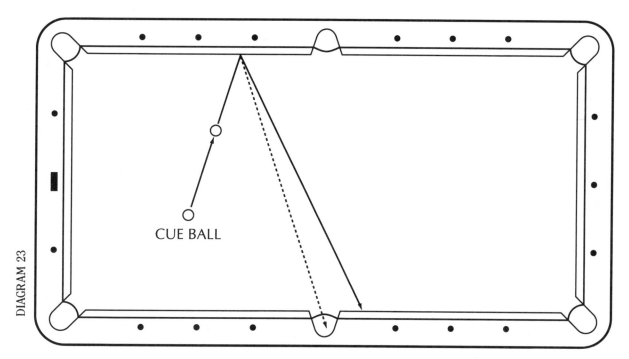

DIAGRAM 23

CUE BALL

If the natural angle of a bank shot sends the object ball just beyond a pocket, a firm stroke will shorten the ball's departure angle.

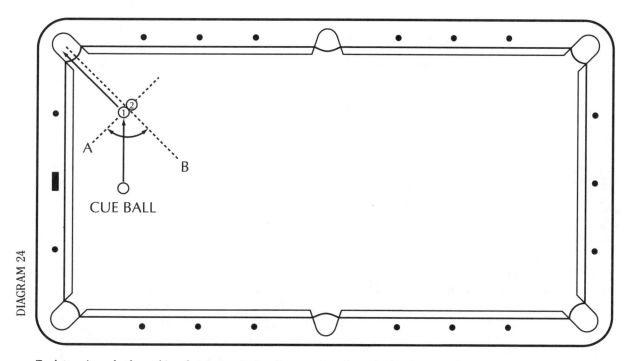

DIAGRAM 24

A

B

CUE BALL

To determine whether a kiss shot is "on," visualize one line through the object balls (A) and another between the balls (B). If the second line runs directly into a pocket, the shot is on.

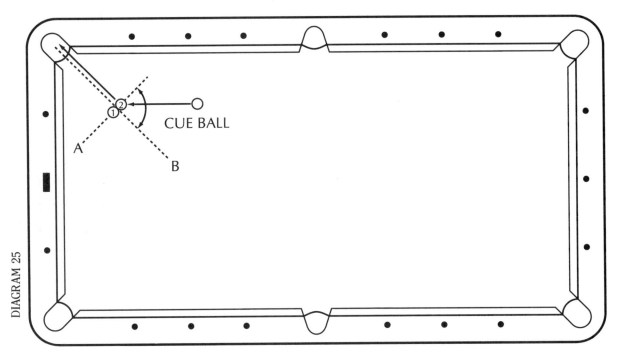

DIAGRAM 25

CUE BALL

A

B

Another look at the same kiss shot, only this time the cue ball is swung around to the other side of the 1-ball and 2-ball. This time, the 2-ball is "on" to the corner pocket.

To determine the feasibility of a kiss shot, make a line directly between the balls. If that line runs into a pocket, the kiss should work.

(courtesy of Carmine R. Manicone Photography)

ball, it's a safe bet your shot will be successful.

Take the same situation, only swing the object ball around to the other side of the 1-ball and 2-ball (Diagram 25). The same principle applies in attempting to pocket the 2-ball.

Combination shots, as the name suggests, are chain-reaction shots involving more than one object ball. "Combos," as beginners love to call them, are deliciously tempting because they're impressive—*when* they work. Again, you're better off looking for another shot unless the combination is perfectly in line with the pocket. And, unless the intended ball is teetering on the edge of a pocket, don't attempt combinations in which the object balls are more than a foot apart.

Diagram 26 shows a dream combination. Unfortunately, these don't come up too often. This is a fairly easy shot to make, because you don't have to adjust your aim to compensate for the second ball. Simply aim the 1-ball as though you were attempting to pocket it in the corner. The 1-ball will strike the 2-ball straight on, and the 2-ball will deposit itself in the corner pocket.

Off-angle combinations, like that shown in Diagram 27, come up far more often. Now your concentration must be on determining where the 1-ball should strike the 2-ball to drive it into the corner pocket. In instances like this, it's best not to worry so much about the corner pocket. Act as though the contact point on the 2-ball is a pocket, and try to "pocket" the 1-ball there.

SHOTS ALONG THE RAIL

Ask five different people how to shoot at a ball frozen to the rail, and you're likely to get five different answers. Some people say you should hit the object ball first. Some say you aim to hit the rail first. Still others suggest you contact the object ball and rail simultaneously.

Try to avoid combination shots unless they are lined up directly to a pocket. The key is to aim the first ball(s) to contact a certain spot on the ball you intend to pocket. Once that spot is determined, forget the pocket and concentrate on hitting the object ball in the right place.

(courtesy of Carmine R. Manicone Photography)

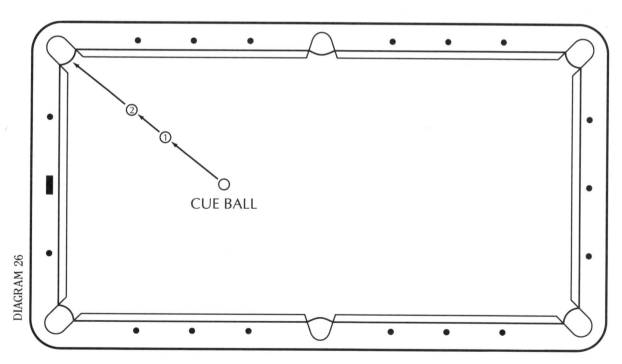

DIAGRAM 26

CUE BALL

In the unlikely event of a straight-on, two-ball combination, aim as though you intend to pocket the 1-ball in the corner.

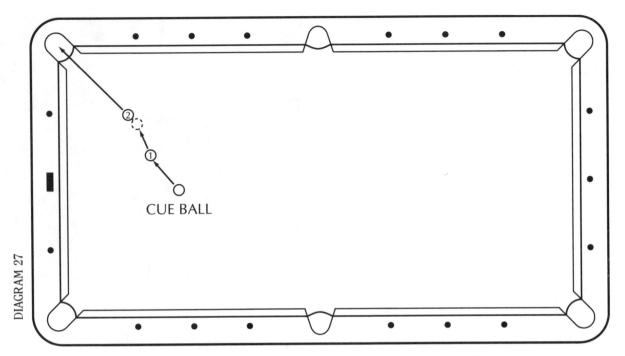

DIAGRAM 27

CUE BALL

On the more common off-angle combination shot, concentrate solely on sending the 1-ball to the proper contact point on the 2-ball. The rest of the shot will take care of itself.

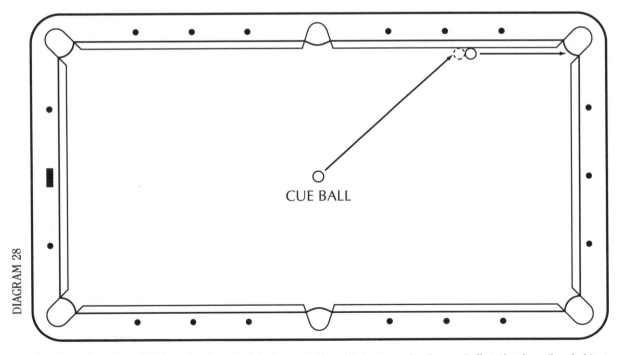

DIAGRAM 28

CUE BALL

On shots along the rail (when the object ball is frozen to the rail), try to make the cue ball strike the rail and object ball simultaneously.

A lot depends on where the cue ball must travel after the hit for position on the next ball. However, if it's the last shot of the game and you don't have to worry about position, I subscribe to the theory that the cue ball must contact the object ball and rail simultaneously (Diagram 28). If you hit the rail first, you're going to kick the ball away from the rail. If you hit the object ball first, you'll drive it into the rail and throw it off course.

APRIL.—The finishing touch

Be aware of people and objects around you. Excessive body English or backswing can adversely affect your game (as well as the games of those around you).

6
Pool Etiquette

Rules, rules, so many rules.

It's not enough to study the rules of the various pool games and memorize the general rules of thumb regarding grip, stroke, stance, etc. When you take your skills to the local billiard room, there are a few more rules that need to be observed.

The standard billiard room rule is "No Gambling." You've seen the sign. It's best to follow this rule, at least to the point of discretion. Wads of money being hurled onto or across a pool table is generally frowned upon by proprietors. If you're compelled to make some kind of wager with your playing partner, consider playing for the table time or for a drink.

Because poolrooms consist of more than one table, be at least semi-conscious of the people around you. Keep your followthrough within the confines of the table area, and keep your body movements to a minimum. Absolutely *no* Tom Cruise "Werewolves of London" imitations!

There may be times you find yourself back-to-back with a player from the next table. Yield to your pool compatriot. Allow him or her to shoot while you give your impending shot selection a second look. More often than not, the player shooting first, cognizant

that you're still waiting to shoot, rushes his or her attempt and misses the shot.

If you don't have your own cue, treat the house cue as you would your own. Don't allow it to drop to the floor, and don't leave it leaning against a wall. Most rooms these days have better-than-average house cues. In fact, many players who bring their own two-piece cues to the poolroom still prefer to break with a slightly heavier, one-piece house cue. The choice is yours.

Finally, to avoid any altercations, be sure the rules of the game you're playing are well understood.

THE SUBTLE ART OF SHARKING

You're hunched over the table, carefully lining up the potential game-winning shot—8-ball in the corner pocket. Your opponent is sitting in a chair near the wall, directly in your line of aim.

You take a few practice strokes. Everything looks perfect.

With the precision of a diamond cutter, you draw your cue straight back.

Just as you're about to make contact with the cue ball, your opponent pulls a

(courtesy of The Billiard Archive)

If you and your partner simply must wager on a game, keep the bet small. How about table time, or a beer? If you lose, be a gentleman and pay your debt.

gleaming white, three-foot-long handkerchief from the pocket of his sport coat!

With a spasmodic lurch, you drive the 8-ball directly into the long rail, a good diamond and a half from the corner pocket.

Your opponent, looking as innocent as a choirboy, genteelly brushes the handkerchief (more like a bedspread) across his nose and returns it to his pocket. He offers his condolences for your untimely miss and proceeds to run the remainder of the balls.

Welcome to the subtle art of sharking.

In pool circles, any movement or action taken to deliberately break the concentration of the shooter is considered sharking. Every player knows how to shark an opponent. Some players, though, are more accomplished than others. In fact, to some aficionados, sharking is an art form.

The key to sharking is to disrupt your opponent's concentration. A player who is really into a groove, all but oblivious to anything outside the confines of the baize-covered table, is said to be "in dead stroke." You can tell when your opponent has gone into this trancelike behavior, and it's a helpless feeling. You know it's going to take an earthquake to snap him out of it. The unethical player will take steps to cause that earthquake.

You're most susceptible to sharking tactics when your opponent is in your line of vision. This is more likely to happen in a poolroom or tavern than in tournament play. In tournaments, when you're not shooting, you're relegated to your chair.

Any kind of quick movement when you're preparing to shoot can cause sufficient distraction. Some of the "standard" moves include the old handkerchief ploy, teetering a cue from hand to hand, taking off a jacket, and standing up suddenly.

Perhaps the most common tactic, but one that requires absolutely perfect timing, is the lighting of a cigarette. As one old player explained: "I'm really in stroke, running balls from everywhere. I can see my opponent is starting to sweat. He's got an unlit cigarette

(courtesy of *Billiards Digest*)

Ronnie Allen is considered to be "Jaws" in the ocean of modern pool sharks.

You never know where a shark might surface. Sometimes, they're in the stands as well as at the pool table.

dangling between his lips, and his lighter is on the table next to him. I get down over a crucial shot, and just as I'm ready to shoot he flicks his Bic! The butane flame from his lighter must have been three feet high! Darn right he was trying to shark me. I know the guy. He doesn't even smoke!"

Another popular, although amateurish, disruption is the Accidental Cue Drop. This also takes impeccable timing. From an upright position, it takes a standard 21-ounce cue stick approximately three seconds to fall like a redwood, striking the floor with a resounding thwack! (Many of the new poolrooms feature plush carpeting. Pity.)

The most fiendish sharking stratagems, however, are those that prey on the subconscious.

When a basketball player is poised to shoot a critical free throw at the end of a game, the opposing team often calls a time-out to make the player think about the importance of the shot. Television analysts refer to it as "icing" the player. The same holds in football, when the kicker is readying himself to attempt the winning field goal.

In pool, which does not utilize time-outs, your opponent may simply retire to the men's room! Not overly creative, but very effective. In fact, the longer he stays away, the more frustrated and out of sync you get.

Reverse psychology can be useful as well.

One such move, which takes place as you approach the game-ending shot, is the seemingly concessionary gesture of your opponent unscrewing his cue. Does this trite little ploy work? Consider that the Men's Professional Billiard Association instituted a rule forbidding a competitor from unscrewing his cue before a match's conclusion.

It should also be noted that in some cases, getting sharked is a self-fulfilling prophecy. If you're absolutely convinced your opponent is (or is going to try) sharking you, your concentration is already shot. Your opponent might sit quietly and not move a muscle the entire match. Afterward, you'll convince yourself that his intention was to shark you by not doing anything.

What sets poolroom sharks of "Jaws" status apart from commonplace sharks is creativity. I've played people who, I discovered later, had strategically "planted" friends in the stands surrounding the table. The direction in which I aimed didn't matter. There was always someone in my line of vision sneezing or knocking an ashtray off the bleachers or lifting a cup to his mouth.

The greatest sharking technique of all time belonged to former carom billiards king Robert Cannefax, who ruled the Three-Cushion billiard roost in the 1920s. Cannefax was a gifted athlete and fierce competitor. As a youth he seemed destined for a career as a major league baseball player, but an injury forced the amputation of his right leg. In its place, Cannefax wore a wooden prosthesis. He then replaced baseball with billiards and excelled almost immediately.

Still intensely competitive, Cannefax loathed losing—or even missing a single shot. As a means of relieving hostility, either after a frustrating miss or while waiting for another turn at the table, Cannefax would sit in his chair and jab himself in the right leg with a pen knife he always carried in his coat pocket.

Not surprisingly, the sight of a man stabbing his leg with a knife managed to unnerve many opponents.

You can even say the ploy gave Cannefax "a leg up" on his competitors. He went on to win five world championships.

7
Straight Pool

It's difficult for me to talk about pocket billiard games without putting Straight Pool at the top of the list.

Straight Pool is also called 14.1 Continuous. Beginners may recognize it as Call Shot. The reason it's called 14.1 Continuous is that, since you have to call every shot to continue, you shoot 14 and leave one ball. After re-racking the other 14, you shoot that one ball in such a manner that the cue ball caroms into the rack and dislodges a few balls. This allows you to continue your run.

When I was growing up, Straight Pool was the main game. It is the supreme test of skill and has been considered the game of champions throughout this century. Only in the past decade or so has Nine-Ball supplanted Straight Pool as the main tournament game.

Most pros agree that a solid Straight Pool background will make you a good player in any pool discipline. A good Straight Pool player can play Nine-Ball or Eight-Ball well. Proficiency at Nine-Ball, though, doesn't presume proficiency at Straight Pool.

The reason is that Straight Pool encompasses all aspects of your pool game—position, shot making, thinking, safety play, and strategy. In a game like Nine-Ball, there are

only nine balls on the table, and their numbers dictate which ball you have to shoot next. In Straight Pool, no two players would likely go through a rack of 15 balls exactly the same way.

Straight Pool, although the most difficult pool game in which to excel, is the easiest for the beginner to start with. Simply throw 15 balls out onto the play field and try to clear the table. You can choose any ball and shoot it into any pocket. It's a great way to learn to think at the table. No decisions are made for you by a ball's number, like in Eight-Ball or Nine-Ball.

THE RULES

Each ball in Straight Pool counts as one point. You must declare the intended object ball and the pocket in which it will end up. (You do not, however, have to specify how many rails it will hit on its way to the pocket or what other balls it will come in contact with along the way.) The object of Straight Pool is to score a predetermined number of points before your opponent. Most championship tournaments play 150-point games, although some extend the finals to 200 points.

To start the game, the 15 object balls are racked in a triangle at the foot spot. The cue ball is placed behind the head string.

OPENING BREAK

On the opening break, the shooter must either call an object ball and the pocket in which he intends to sink it, or he can choose a "safe" break. The only requirements are that he drive at least two object balls to a cushion and that the cue ball strike a cushion after contact with an object ball. Failure to meet these requirements is a two-point penalty. (The deduction of penalty points can result in negative scores in Straight Pool.) The opponent has the option of accepting the table as it is or having the balls re-racked and making his opponent break again. If the shooter scratches on the break, it is a foul, and he is penalized one point. Three consecutive fouls results in a 15-point penalty. (Some tournaments have made the three-foul penalty 20 percent of the total balls needed to win. That's 30 points in a 150-point match, which is pretty steep!)

On each shot, a player must cause the cue ball to contact an object ball, then pocket an object ball or cause the cue ball or any object ball to contact a cushion. Failure to do so is a foul and one-point penalty.

When only one object ball remains on the table, the other 14 balls are re-racked with the space at the foot spot left vacant in the triangle (Diagram 29). The shooter may then pocket the fifteenth ball (also called the *break ball*) in such a manner as to send the cue ball into the rack and bump several object balls into the open. He may, however, call a safety rather than an object ball. The safety must still comply with the rules stated above to be allowed.

These are the very basic rules for Straight Pool. For rulings on balls that leave the table, break balls which interfere with the re-racking of the other 14 balls, and other unusual circumstances, consult the Billiard

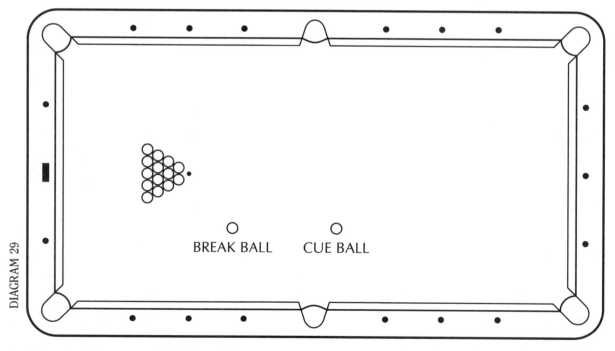

DIAGRAM 29

BREAK BALL   CUE BALL

When the balls are re-racked in Straight Pool, the space at the apex of the triangle is left open.

THIS GUINNESS RECORD IS STOUT!

For some reason, endurance records have always intrigued people. Record-seekers constantly attempt to establish new marks in virtually every and any conceivable activity—dance marathons, roller-skating marathons, rope-skipping contests, etc. Pool is no different.

The record for most balls pocketed in a 24-hour period more than doubled from 1974 to 1981. In 1974, a self-proclaimed champion named "Superstroke" Bruce Christopher set the mark of 5,688 balls. Four years later, 25-year-old Pearl Harbor signalman Robert Hayward eclipsed the mark by canning 8,246 balls. (That's roughly one rack every three minutes.)

Hayward's record lasted just over a year, when professional player Mike "Tennessee Tarzan" Massey utilized side-by-side tables to set a new record—10,020 balls!

On July 1, 1979, a new record was set in New Zealand. Gary Maunsey of Hamilton, New Zealand, tagged another 1,700 balls onto the old mark. His total of 11,700 balls in less than 24 hours breaks down to one ball every 7.38 seconds, and that's not counting missed shots!

Congress of America's *Official Rules and Record Book*.

PLAYING STRAIGHT POOL

The opening break in Straight Pool is critical. Goof up, and you may not get to shoot again! The opening break is a defensive shot. It's almost impossible to declare a specific ball to be pocketed on the break. And you certainly don't want to scatter the balls all over the table. In fact, you don't want to leave your opponent *any* shot.

Something to be very careful about, and this holds true in all pocket billiard games, is making sure the balls in the rack are frozen before you break. When the balls aren't frozen, they tend to scatter in unpredictable directions.

If given the option, you always want your opponent to break in Straight Pool. However, if you must break, set the cue ball along the head string between the head spot

(courtesy of Carmine R. Manicone Photography)

You'll be hard pressed to find any better opening break in Straight Pool than this. The cue ball is glued to the head rail, and the balls have virtually been re-racked. Your shot!

All break shots in Straight Pool should be so perfect! A nice angle on a very makeable shot. No need to smash the balls—a normal stroke will dislodge plenty of balls without risk of losing control of the cue ball.
(courtesy of Carmine R. Manicone Photography)

When the angle on the break ball is this severe, you will need to use "follow" on the cue ball. Not many players enjoy following the cue ball into the rack. There are too many potential pitfalls.
(courtesy of Carmine R. Manicone Photography)

With break shots that have a very slight angle, you risk not getting the cue ball into the rack at all. A little "draw" on this shot will improve your chances of bringing the cue ball back to the middle of the table.
(courtesy of Carmine R. Manicone Photography)

and the side rail. Using a relatively soft stroke, try to clip the ball at the corner of the rack on the same side of the table from which you are breaking (Diagram 30). Properly hit, the cue ball will glance off the object ball to the bottom rail, over to the side rail, and back up to the cushion at the head of the table.

Meanwhile, the corner ball will hit the bottom rail and return to the edge of the rack. The corner ball on the opposite side of the rack should move directly to the side rail and back near its original position.

Voila! You've fulfilled your requirements (two object balls hit a rail, as did the cue ball after contacting an object ball), and your opponent is in deep trouble. Now he, most likely, will have to attempt to play safe also.

SAFETY PLAY

Because the top Straight Pool players are so skillful and capable of runs well over 100, safety play is very important. You never want to leave a good player an open rack at which to shoot. Unless you are certain you have a shot, it's always best to play safe.

The path to a good safety begins with the admission that you're going to give up the table. No player enjoys sitting down during a Straight Pool match, because there is no guarantee that you'll get back to the table before the game is over. I've seen many players push their luck by trying a difficult shot—and pay the price for missing and leaving their opponent even a slim chance to break out. (I've been guilty of this infraction plenty of times!)

As your run gets longer and longer, convincing yourself to play a safety gets more and more difficult. Knowing when to run and when to hide becomes a mind game. Use your head. A lot of players get caught up with high runs. Don't concern yourself with that. What good is a run of 112 if you leave an open table and your opponent runs 150-and-out?

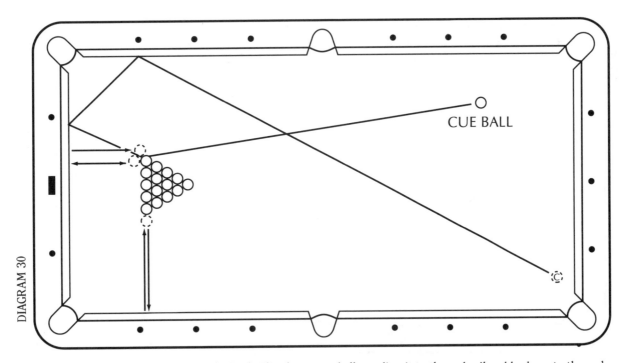

DIAGRAM 30

The perfect opening break in Straight Pool. Clip the corner ball, sending it to the end rail and back up to the rack. The object ball in the opposite corner will roll to the side rail and back near the bottom of the rack. Meanwhile, the cue ball will travel two rails and back up to the head rail.

Players who consistently run 30 or 40 balls (it may take a beginner a year or two to run 30) are solid players. In championship play, the average balls-per-inning is about 15. If you can run 35, then play safe, get back to the table, and run another 40, you'll be fine. Play within yourself. When the table is open, make the shots. When things get a little tight, play safe and don't risk giving your opponent an open table.

Once you've established the fact that you're going to play safe, look over the entire table carefully. Don't get too cute. Find a situation that will allow you to play a legal shot, and leave your opponent with the cue ball in an undesirable position. On the opening break, this is accomplished by sending the cue ball to the head rail. In the post-break stages, it is more common to bury the cue ball in a cluster of balls or directly behind an object ball that has no chance of being pocketed.

If you find yourself in a situation that demands safety play, look for frozen combinations that will suit your needs. Here, I see that the 7-, 15-, and 13-balls are conveniently frozen in a line to the end rail.
(courtesy of Carmine R. Manicone Photography)

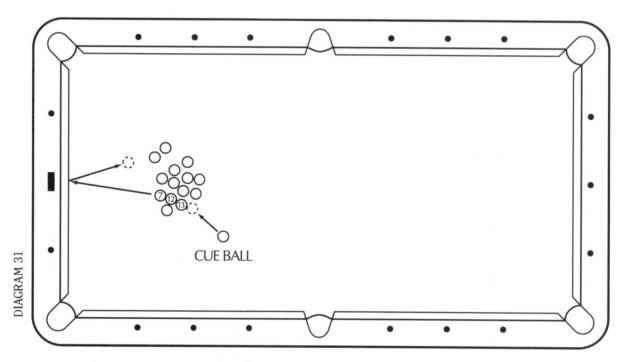

DIAGRAM 31

CUE BALL

A very simple yet effective safety in Straight Pool is to stick the cue ball to a frozen cluster. In this case, a very delicate touch on the 13-ball will cause the 7-ball to react down to the bottom rail. Your opponent is left with no shot.

Diagram 31 (and the accompanying photographs) shows a rack that has barely been disturbed. After examining the rack for any "dead" shots (kisses or combinations that line up directly to a pocket), you concede that a safety is in order. In this instance, the 13-ball, 12-ball, and 7-ball are frozen. Because they are frozen, you don't have to concern yourself with errant kiss-offs. By simply nudging the 13-ball, the chain reaction will send the 7-ball to the bottom rail. Don't worry about where the 7-ball winds up. Your only concern is hitting the cue ball just hard enough to get the 7-ball to the rail and leave the cue ball glued to the 13-ball. Most safety play requires a very delicate touch.

Safety play is also fairly common after a break shot on which the cue ball fails to contact the stack. With the rack still intact, your run is pretty much over. Time again to play a safety. Since you checked the rack before your break shot and found the balls to

By hitting the cue ball into the 7-ball (delicately!), the 13-ball rolled to the end rail—fulfilling my shot requirement—and the cue ball remained nuzzled in the rack. Your shot again!
(courtesy of Carmine R. Manicone Photography)

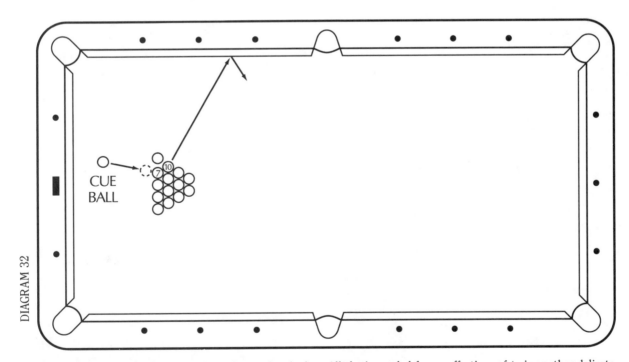

DIAGRAM 32

CUE BALL

Sometimes, the cue ball misses the rack on a break shot. All that's needed for an effective safety is another delicate center ball hit on a frozen combination. By tapping the 7-ball, the 10-ball will squirt out to the side rail. The cue ball and 7-ball remain in place, leaving a tough situation for your opponent.

be frozen, playing safe here is pretty easy (Diagram 32). All that's needed is a delicate stop shot on the first ball in the combination. In this case, strike the 7-ball. The 10-ball will pop out of the stack toward the side rack. The cue ball remains stuck to the bottom of the stack.

There will be some instances, unfortunately, in which no perfect safety is available. Rather than taking a risky shot or playing a poor safety, don't discount the benefit of an intentional foul. By gently nudging the cue ball into the rack, you may not send an object ball to a rail, thus committing a foul and losing one point. But isn't that better than

playing a senseless shot and watching your opponent run 50 or 60 balls? Just remember that three consecutive fouls results in a much more severe penalty, so if you intentionally foul on two consecutive shots, be ready to absolve yourself on the third shot.

BREAK SHOTS

Perhaps the only part of Straight Pool that involves some luck is the break shot. When you pocket the break ball and the cue ball dives into the rack, there is no telling what will happen. When 14 balls and a cue ball begin to scatter and bump into each other, you just hold your breath and hope for the

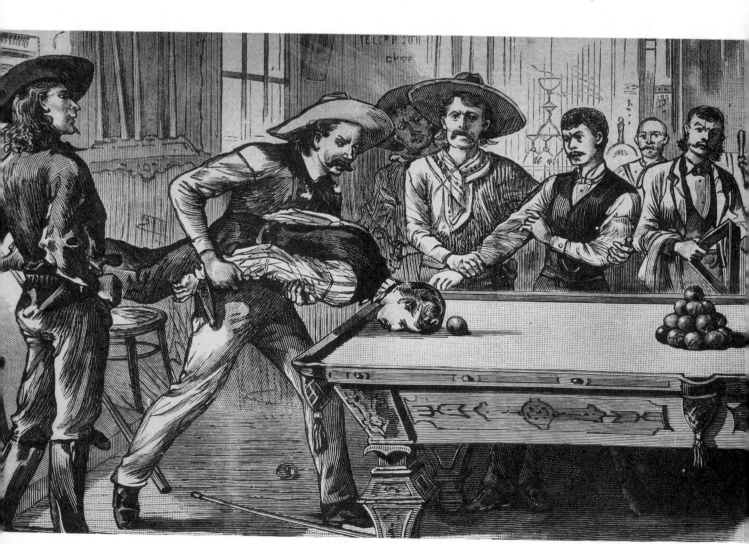

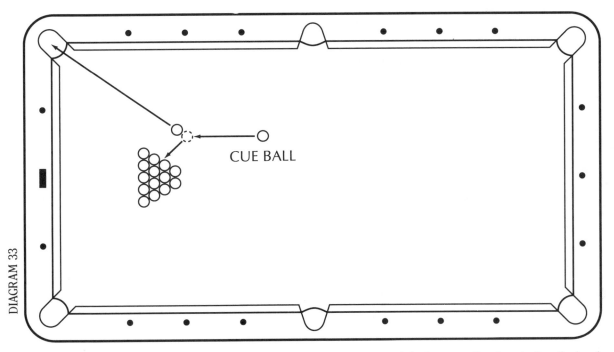

DIAGRAM 33

CUE BALL

The most favorable break shot in Straight Pool is made by shooting toward the bottom rail and pocketing the break ball in one of the corner pockets.

best. You're never certain where the cue ball will end up. Will you have another shot? Or will the cue ball be hopelessly trapped behind or inside a cluster of balls?

There are, however, ways you can increase the odds of having the cue ball wind up in a favorable spot. First, on break shots that don't require a severe cut on the object ball, it's best to draw the cue ball into the stack. Because the cue ball has reverse spin on it, it will tend to hit the stack and retreat to the open table. With follow, the cue ball might slide off the stack to the bottom of the table or burrow its way farther into the stack. The more congestion, the more likely the cue ball is to run into trouble.

For break shots that lie on a severe angle (hitting less than half the object ball), I usually use follow.

Shooting toward the bottom rail and

pocketing the break ball in one of the corner pockets are the most favorable break shots (Diagram 33). Shots of this nature allow you to draw the cue ball away from trouble. Personally, I try to avoid break shots from beneath the rack (Diagram 34). You're sending the cue ball into the meat of the stack, where there is a better than average chance the cue ball will find itself surrounded by hostile object balls.

RUNNING BALLS

Obviously, the break ball doesn't simply appear. You have to play toward the break ball, which gets us back to the topic of position play. You have to think ahead, but don't be intimidated by players who insist that pros have the entire rack planned before the first object ball is pocketed. That's just not true.

When there are 10 or more balls on the table in Straight Pool, position play entails no more than thinking two or three balls in advance. There are two points to be wary of. First, always have an alternative plan. It's

◀ Some players prefer to break with a heavier cue. Try to keep your choice of cues within reason.
(courtesy of The Billiard Archive)

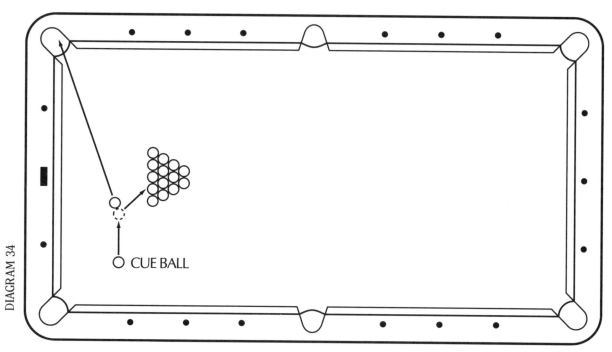

DIAGRAM 34

CUE BALL

I try to avoid Straight Pool break shots from below the rack. Too often, the cue ball tends to get buried in the bottom of the stack.

easy to say, "I'm going to pocket the 4-ball, then the 6, the 12, the 15, etc." What if you get out of line after the first ball? Did you pick a ball that left you no alternatives? If, however, you have to get to a certain ball, you have to be a little more perfect. Also, if you see a likely candidate for your break shot, avoid it like the plague! Don't risk bumping it out of position.

The primary task in Straight Pool is to avoid missing. Other keys are breaking up clusters and taking care of trouble balls—balls along the rail, at the head of the table, etc. If you have 12 balls on one end of the table, and two on the upper end, take care of the two on the upper end as soon as possible and come back down for the other 12. Look the table over right away to determine where potential problems exist. Try to eliminate those trouble areas as quickly as possible.

One common trouble area is clusters—balls that are frozen or nearly frozen in a small grouping (Diagram 35). Don't try to

break them loose on your first shot. Be patient and keep your eyes open for a ball that will allow you to reach that cluster naturally. You can already see that by pocketing the 7-ball with a delicate center ball hit, the angle presented by the 10-ball will allow the cue ball easy access to the cluster. As you become a smarter player, you'll notice that sending the cue ball to the top of the cluster adds a little insurance to the shot. The cue ball will glance slightly toward the center of the table, free of harm's way.

When breaking up clusters and trouble spots, there's no need to slam the balls. Just a little nudge will do the trick.

Another thing. If the table is relatively open, bumping into balls with the cue ball is a bad habit. You may nudge one ball into another or push one to the rail. It's tough enough cleaning up the trouble areas that already exist. Don't create more problems by being careless with the cue ball. The fewer balls you hit while playing position, the bet-

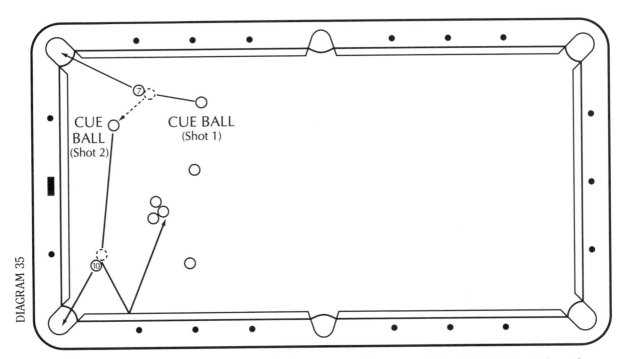

DIAGRAM 35

Since you never slam the cue ball into the stack, clusters are fairly common in Straight Pool. Don't force the cue ball into a cluster. Play prudently toward a ball which gives you a safe, natural angle to the trouble area. In this case, a delicate center ball hit on the 7-ball gives you an opportunity to break up the cluster from the 10-ball.

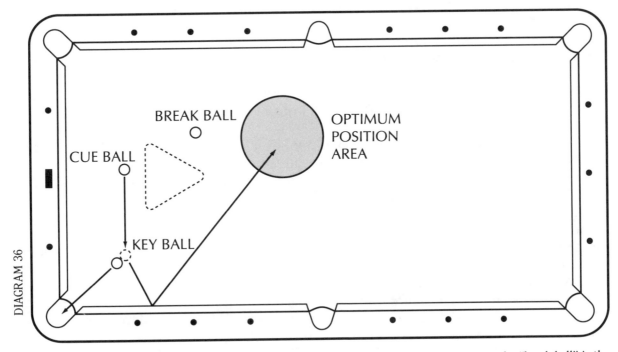

DIAGRAM 36

The "key ball" is the next to last ball in a rack. Maneuvering from the key ball to position on the "break ball" is the difference between running 14 balls and several racks.

ter. If you have to move balls, be sure you have some approximation of where they are headed.

As you approach the end of a rack, you'll come up on the key ball—the second to last ball left on the table. It is referred to this way because position of the key ball determines whether your break shot will be effective. Maneuvering from key ball to break ball is the difference between running one rack of balls and running multiple racks.

The position on the key ball in Diagram 36 is nearly perfect. A normal center ball, or slightly below center, hit on the cue ball will leave you in fine shape for the break shot. Again, don't try to be too perfect. Play to send the cue ball to an imaginary zone or circle. Anywhere in the circle shown in the diagram will be sufficient. Just make sure the cue ball goes beyond straight-in on the break ball. You must have an angle from which to break open the rack.

I still believe Straight Pool is the best game for beginners, because it helps you develop a balanced, well-rounded game. This point is obvious even at the professional level. The pros who honed their skills on Straight Pool are near the top of the Nine-Ball rankings year after year. Their game seems to hold up over a longer period of time than born-and-bred Nine-Ballers.

MY RISE AS A PLAYER

Although I was considered a kind of prodigy around the pool table, my ascent to pool's elite upper echelon was a bit different from that of most players.

By the time I was 11, I had already run more than 50 consecutive balls in Straight Pool. Upon reaching the age of 13, I topped the century mark and won the city championship. I played in the New Jersey State Championship every year throughout my teens.

But I do believe that during my peak years—late teens and through my twenties—I was at a huge disadvantage. Despite being one of the top players, I was also one of only a handful of players who held a steady job. With the exception of about three months during my adult life, I was either a full-time student or a full-time teacher. And, incredibly, during that three-month period I didn't hold a steady job, my game went downhill!

The reason I always worked is simple: pool didn't offer much of a livelihood back then. And the life of a pool player on the road is not really all that glamorous.

In the late sixties and early seventies, a big tournament might have a top prize of $5,000, with maybe $2,500 for third. At the beginning, I finished second and third a few times and thought, "Gee, this is pretty easy." That's when I decided to take a three-month leave from my teaching job. I played everywhere, but all of a sudden I was finishing eighteenth and nineteenth. That was usually worth $150 here and $100 there. Back to work!

My job? School teacher. I graduated from Athens State College in Athens, Alabama, with an education degree. In 1968 I started teaching seventh grade history at Perth Amboy Grammar School, which later became William McGinnis Junior High School. It was a terrific job, and I taught there for 13 years.

One of the job's few drawbacks was the five-day workweek. If there was a tournament in Norfolk, Virginia, I would make the six-hour drive on a Tuesday evening

Winning my first BCA U.S. Open championship in 1970 was easily the greatest single moment I've had in the game. Winning the sport's most prestigious tournament, at age 27, gave me a feeling I'll never really be able to describe adequately. (courtesy of *Billiards Digest*)

(courtesy of *Billiards Digest*)

to play and then drive back to New Jersey for class on Wednesday morning. I always had friends drive with me. I'd pay their way, and they would do the driving on the way home so that I could get some sleep. I would drive back to Norfolk on Thursday after school to play a few more matches, then, I'd take Friday off.

It was during those years, however, that I had some of my greatest moments as a professional player. Actually, my first great moment came in 1964, when I finished second to Irving "Deacon" Crane in the Tournament of Champions television series. It was my first major competition, and it featured some of the very best players of the day.

My most dominant years as a player began in 1969. I won four major tournaments that year—the Stardust Open, the Salt Lake City Open, the New Jersey Open, and the U.S. Masters. I successfully defended my New Jersey and U.S. Masters titles in 1970, and then came the Billiard Congress of America U.S. Open 14.1 Championship.

The BCA U.S. Open was the most prestigious tournament in pool. I was playing great pool then and met the late, great Luther "Wimpy" Lassiter in the championship match. Luther was one of the game's greatest all-around players and was quite a character. He always seemed to have some kind of ailment, and he'd moan and groan and look like he could barely stand up—all the while drilling one ball after the next into pockets. He was fabulous. He was also the defending U.S. Open champ.

I remember the match like it was yesterday. I remember finding an opening early in the match and running 102 balls, then scratching. It was incredible. I really think if I hadn't scratched I would have run out. I had to sit there and watch Lassiter run 80-something balls. Then, after one of his many delays to retire to the men's room, he missed a simple little break shot. I'll never forget seeing that. I jumped clear out of my chair and ran 47-and-out.

I was so happy. I was totally in tears. People kept coming up to me and saying, "What's the matter?" They just didn't understand what that meant to me and what that felt like. It was, by far, the greatest feeling I ever had in pool. It always will be, too.

I went on to win the next three BCA U.S. Open championships, and captured many more titles in the seventies. The latter part of that decade, though, was one of the toughest periods of my life. I had a few personal problems, and players began to doubt my ability at the table. They thought my time had passed.

One tournament I had failed to win in the late seventies was the PPPA World Open 14.1 Championship. It had replaced the BCA U.S. Open as pool's premier event. Despite, or perhaps because of, my newfound fame and fortune, I had a burning desire to win that tournament. It would prove a lot to the other players and, frankly, to myself.

I made a comeback for the sole reason of winning the 1982 World Open, and I was successful. I defeated another great player, Danny DiLiberto, in the finals. While the 1970 BCA U.S. Open was my greatest moment in pool, winning the 1982 World Open was my most satisfying moment. Winning again in 1983 helped dismiss any thoughts that I was lucky in 1982. I felt I had made a statement.

Since then I've continued to play competitively, mostly because I like competition and still feel I can win. Once you've devoted a portion of your life to head-to-head competition, I don't think you ever really lose the competitive fire. You see it in all sports, when star players continue to play long after they've reached financial security. Why? Competitive fire.

(photo by Billie Billing)

Competitive drive is something I've never lost. I still feel I can win any tournament I enter, and I'll continue to play until I feel otherwise. I love a challenge.

The standard Eight-Ball rack needs only to have the 8-ball in the middle, and a stripe and a solid in opposite corners. The remainder of the balls may be randomly racked.

8
Eight-Ball

Eight-Ball (also called Stripes & Solids, Bigs & Littles, Highs & Lows, etc.) is far and away the most universally known pool game. According to various companies that survey sports participation, between 23 and 31 million Americans enjoy a game of billiards at least once each year. It's a safe bet that the vast majority of those participants play Eight-Ball.

One of the largest growth areas in billiards over the past five years has been the ground swell of activity at the grass roots level. Much in the same manner that bowling leagues helped fortify the bowling industry, organized tavern pool leagues have managed to generate a broad base of enthusiastic, committed billiards participants.

Today, nearly half a million Americans play in some form of organized Eight-Ball league. Several established national pool league groups boast memberships in excess of seventy thousand dues-paying players. While national championship tournaments exist for these leagues, the basic draw is a relaxing evening of socializing—with a little competition thrown in.

In virtually every tavern pool league, Eight-Ball is the game being played. The major reason is that tavern pool consists mainly of play on coin-operated tables. Once a ball is pocketed, there is no way to return it to the table without slotting more money into the table's coin box. For that reason, a rotation-type game, like Nine-Ball, is not practical. A game of Straight Pool would cost a fortune!

The fact that most tavern tables are coin-operated has also had an effect on the rules of the game. No pocket billiard game wears as many faces as Eight-Ball. The number of rule interpretations is staggering. In fact, after traveling around a bit, you get the impression that every establishment in which Eight-Ball is played features its own set of house rules. It's always healthy to inquire about such rules whenever you're about to play a game of Eight-Ball.

THE RULES[1]

Eight-Ball is played with all 15 object balls and the cue ball. The game begins with the object balls racked in a triangle at the foot spot. The only requirements of ball placement within the rack are the 8-ball must be in the center and a solid-colored ball (numbers 1 through 7) must occupy one of the corner

---

1. Rules as established by the Billiard Congress of America.

(courtesy of *Billiards Digest*)

⁘ BEHIND THE 8-BALL? ⁘

If pool's most universally known term is, indeed, "behind the 8-ball," the term must also then rank as the game's most misinterpreted phrase.

The general perception of "behind the 8-ball" is that the term is analogous with "thwarted" or "stymied." It has long been suspected that the connotation derives from the game of Eight-Ball, in which the shooter is not allowed to use the 8-ball in a combination shot. Thus, if a shooter's cue ball is positioned "behind the 8-ball," he is left without an open shot.

In reality, the phrase predates the game of Eight-Ball by at least 20 years. The first set of rules for Eight-Ball were written around 1945, and billiard historians have uncovered usage of the term "behind the 8-ball" as early as 1919.

So what does the term actually mean?

The late billiard champion Charles Peterson once said that the term evolved from a form of rotation pool called "Kelly Pool." A multiplayer game using 15 object balls, Kelly Pool begins with players choosing a numbered "pill" from a shaker bottle. At each stroke, the lowest numbered ball on the table must be contacted first. A player wins by pocketing the ball corresponding to his number, which he keeps secret until his ball is pocketed. If a player's ball is pocketed by another participant, he is eliminated from the game.

If there are seven players, it is possible that each of them may have to shoot at some ball other than his own on the first round, if, for example, the players draw numbers 9–15 and nobody sinks more than one ball. With eight or more players, however, someone will probably have the opportunity to shoot directly at his own ball before any player has a second chance to play, or he will have eliminated the player "behind the 8-ball" (again, because eight is more than half of 15).

As a practical matter, then, a player who has a position worse than eight in the order ("behind the 8-ball") has virtually no chance to win because at least one of his predecessors will have had a shot at the game ball. So the "8-ball" in this context refers not to an object ball, but to one of the Kelly pills.

positions at the bottom of the rack, while a striped ball (numbers 9 through 15) occupies the opposite corner position. The remaining balls can be racked at random.

The object of Eight-Ball is that one player must pocket the striped balls, while the other player must shoot the solid-colored balls. The first player to pocket all the balls of his group, then legally pocket the 8-ball, wins the game.

OPENING BREAK

For the opening break in Eight-Ball, the player breaking may place the cue ball anywhere behind the head string. The cue ball is not required to contact the apex ball first. However, for a break to be considered "legal," the shooter must either pocket an object ball or drive at least four object balls to the rail. If the player pockets a ball on the break and hasn't committed a cue ball foul (scratching or sending the cue ball sailing off the table), he may continue shooting.

Contrary to popular belief, pocketing the 8-ball on the break does not constitute a win for the shooter. If the 8-ball goes in on the break, the shooter can either call for a re-rack and break again, or he can choose to have the 8-ball spotted on the foot spot. Either way, the shooter remains at the table.

CHOICE OF GROUP

The choice of group is determined by the first "called" ball to be pocketed. The table is still open following the break shot, regardless of how many stripes and/or solids have been pocketed.

Also, until choice of group is determined, the shooter can use the 8-ball or a striped ball to sink a solid, and vice versa. Once your group has been established, initial contact must be on a ball from your group.

LOSS OF GAME

There are a host of ways in which the shooter can lose the game. The most common is by pocketing the 8-ball out of turn. It is also a loss of game if the shooter fouls while pocketing the 8-ball (scratches, etc.) or scratches while shooting at the 8-ball. Pocketing the 8-ball in any pocket other than the pocket called by the shooter constitutes a loss of game.

Finally, the shooter may not pocket his final object ball and the 8-ball on the same shot. That is also a loss of game.

(illustration by Terry Luc)

(courtesy of The Billiard Archive)

Confusion over the rules has been known to result in rather lengthy, er, discussions. Remember, you're paying an hourly rate for the table time!

Situation	Official BCA Rule	Popular Social Convention
1. You make the 8-ball on the break.	Shooter has option of re-racking and breaking again, or spotting the 8-ball and accepting the table layout as is.	Shooter wins game. (In some places, the shooter *loses*!)
2. Shooter pockets a stripe or solid on the break.	Table is "open." Shooter may call a ball of either group. If he successfully pockets the called ball, he is restricted to that group, and his opponent must shoot the balls of the other group. If shooter fails to pocket a called ball, the table remains open.	Shooter is restricted to the group of balls which went in on the break. If a ball from each group was pocketed, shooter has the option. If two stripes and one solid went in on the break, shooter must take stripes.
3. Shooter calls the ball he intends to pocket.	Shooter must simply make the ball in the intended pocket.	Shooter must declare if intended ball will contact another ball or rail en route to the pocket.
4. Shooter pockets a ball of his group illegally.	On a coin-operated table, the pocketed ball stays down. On open tables, the ball is spotted.	Ball stays down.
5. Shooter is attempting to pocket the 8-ball.	Shooter must declare the intended pocket, and any contact with a rail or opponent's ball(s).	Shooter must bank the 8-ball to a pocket. = or = Shooter must sink the 8-ball in the same pocket as his final object ball.
6. Shooter scratches on 8-ball.	Shooter loses.	Opponent gets cue ball anywhere behind the head string. = or = Opponent gets cue-ball-in-hand anywhere on the table.

No matter where you play a game of Eight-Ball, you're bound to run into a rule you've never heard of. "House rules" they're called. It may just be coincidence, but you usually seem to find out about these rules near the end of a game you thought you were winning!

To avoid this somewhat frustrating occurrence, it's always advisable to go over the rules before you lean into the opening break.

The "official rules" of Eight-Ball are generally considered to be those specified by the Billiard Congress of America. The previous page lists some common Eight-Ball situations, along with the official BCA ruling. Also listed are several popular rules governing the same situations.

How do your "house rules" differ?

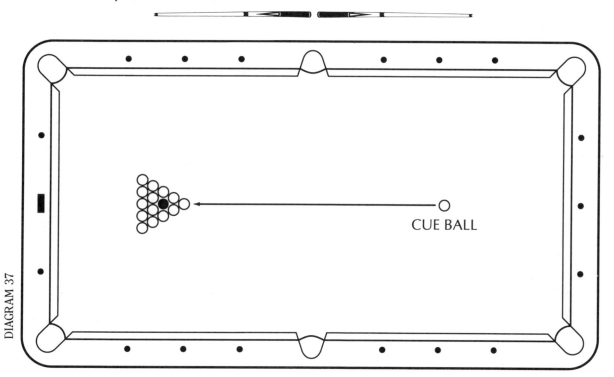

DIAGRAM 37

Players used to break head-on in Eight-Ball, contacting the apex ball flush and as hard as possible.

PLAYING EIGHT-BALL

THE BREAK SHOT

The break shot in Eight-Ball has changed somewhat in recent years. Most players used to break head-on, contacting the apex ball flush and trying to pocket as many balls as possible (Diagram 37). Since most people play by the rule that sinking the 8-ball on the break wins the game, most players break with the cue ball near the side rail. Using draw and

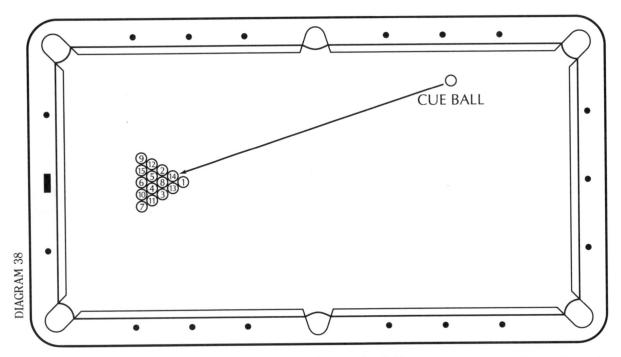

CUE BALL

DIAGRAM 38

Today, the 8-ball break is generally from the side rail to the second ball. This creates more action from balls on the opposite side of the rack, which increases the number of collisions between balls.

aiming for the second ball, you tend to get more action on the 8-ball (Diagram 38) because balls on the opposite side of the rack travel to the side rail and back toward the stack. The more balls that bump into the 8-ball, the greater the chance is it will get pushed toward a pocket. Draw will keep the cue ball from scratching into the corner pocket by swinging it to the side rail and back to the middle of the table.

Because you're dealing with a full rack of balls and trying to scatter them all over the table on the break, there is greater likelihood that the cue ball will run into problems if not kept in the middle of the table. If you decide to break head-on, use just a touch of draw on the cue ball. There's no need to use extreme draw, because the impact of the cue ball into the apex ball will cause it to jump back anyway.

HOW TO CHOOSE THE RIGHT GROUP

The determination of groups may be the most common misconception in Eight-Ball. I think the official ruling is fair for several reasons. First, even though a striped ball went in on the break, I may not want stripes. The layout of the solids might be more favorable. Why should I be forced, by the luck of the break, to take stripes? Also, if I make a stripe on the break (sheer luck), but miss my first shot, why should my opponent be forced to take solids? I've yet to sink a ball I intended to pocket.

Whenever you approach a table that is still open, survey the entire layout carefully. One of the most frequent mistakes players make in Eight-Ball is automatically going for the easiest opening shot. Some beginners do this because they aren't used to thinking ahead. Others are afraid they'll look foolish if they fail to make a ball when the table is open.

Be smart. Instead of immediately looking for the easiest shot, look for trouble areas. The table layout in Diagram 39 is somewhat exaggerated, but it proves a point. As tempting as the 13-ball is, you're far better off

(courtesy of Carmine R. Manicone Photography)

Most professionals break from the side rail in Eight-Ball. Aim for the second ball and "draw" the cue ball to the side rail—away from trouble.

(courtesy of Carmine R. Manicone Photography)

What should you choose? Solids? Before you decide, take a good look at the 12-ball, which is stuck in a cluster with two solid-colored balls. The 13-ball gives you a nice chance to break the 12 out of there right away. Take the stripes, and play the 13 to the corner immediately, sending the cue ball over to the side rail to free the 12. Then you're on your way!

choosing solids and trying to pocket the 1-ball in the side pocket. The stripes present a myriad of problems. For starters, there are two troublesome clusters of striped balls. Based on the positioning of the other striped balls, the two-ball cluster along the side rail will be extremely difficult to reach. And breaking the three-ball cluster near the foot spot brings the 8-ball into play. Bumping into the 8-ball is risky business indeed. Dump these problems off on your opponent!

The 1-ball may be a slightly more difficult shot, but making it will allow you to gain position on the balls at the upper end of the table. Then you can move down the table for the other three solids and the 8-ball. (Naturally, you'd better make the 1-ball, or your opponent will certainly gain the upper hand.)

Another example is the layout left in Diagram 40. What should you choose? Right away, I see a few trouble areas. A cluster along the side rail has one striped ball (the 12) between two solids. Take the stripes, but in doing so realize that you'll need to free that striped ball in the cluster. Try to take care of that right away. Shoot the 13-ball first, and in the process bump the 12-ball loose.

As in Straight Pool, the game of Eight-Ball also has a "key" ball—the final ball of your grouping. As you shoot through your family of balls, keep your eyes open for a ball that will allow you easy access to the 8-ball. The worst thing you can do is pocket the final ball of your group and not leave yourself a shot at the 8-ball. You may be forced to take a risky shot on the 8-ball or leave your opponent the luxury of shooting at his group without any of your balls in the way. That's a huge advantage. So huge, in fact, that I've offered people the following proposition: I get to break, after which all of the balls of one group are removed from the table. My opponent is credited with those balls. I get to continue shooting. Who has the advantage? Me! With

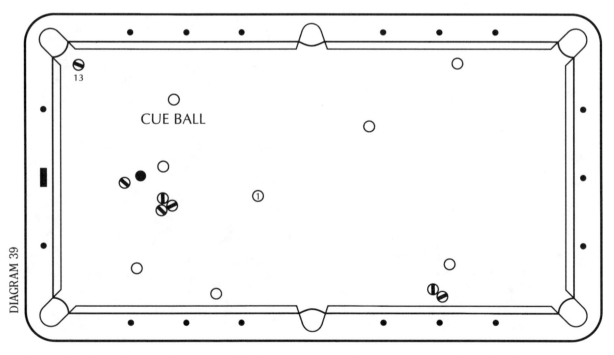

Before choosing stripes and shooting the 13-ball, consider the problems that lie ahead. The solids offer a much easier path. Even though the 1-ball is a tougher shot, it's worth the risk.

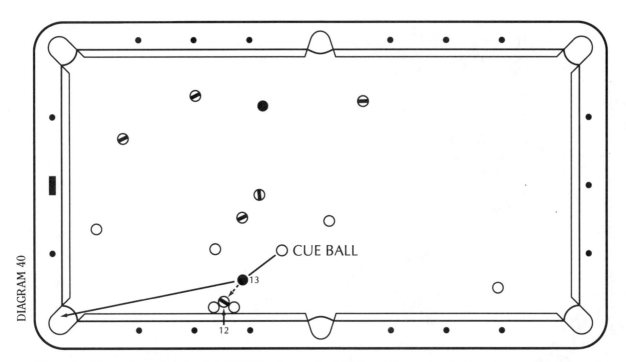

DIAGRAM 40

CUE BALL

13

12

What should you choose? Stripes? Solids? The cluster should tell you that stripes is the proper option. Shoot the 13-ball and bump the 12-ball into the open right away.

none of his balls interfering, I can fire away. Plus, I can play safe, leaving him with no shot at the 8-ball. More times than not, I will win the game.

The last ball in your group is so important, in fact, that unless you have a good

chance of gaining position on the 8-ball, it's better to play safe than to make the ball. Bide your time if need be. Your opponent may give you a better opportunity than you could give yourself.

A BILLIARD MARVEL

Stories of handicapped people playing pool are not uncommon, but few tales can match that of "Handless George" Sutton.

Born in 1870, Sutton lost both hands in a sawmill accident when he was just eight years old. Despite his handicap, he was determined to study medicine and was graduated from the College of Medicine in Milwaukee in 1901. During his college years, Sutton took up the game of billiards. He became so proficient at the game that he established an 18.2 Balkline record by running 799 in 1921.

Sutton took his playing exhibitions on the road and toured for nearly 35 years, astonishing crowds with his skills and his resolve.

He died of a heart attack in Toledo, Ohio, in 1938.

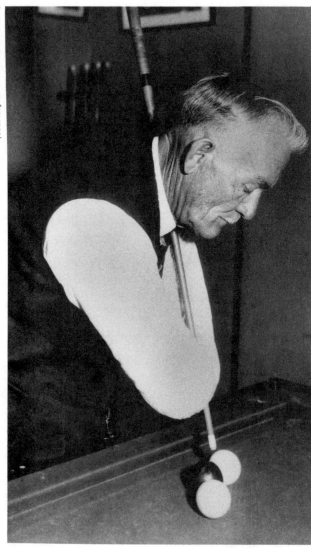

Despite his handicap, George Sutton set records for Balkline and successfully toured the country performing billiard exhibitions.

Remember, unless you are certain you can run out, don't try. The more balls you take off the table, the better your opponent's chances of running out once he comes to the table. When making your choice between trying to run out and playing safe, always think about the consequences. If your attempt to run out comes up short, will your opponent have an open table? Or are there several trouble areas that will make a run-out tough for him regardless of your miss?

In Diagram 41, you really don't have much chance of pocketing the 7-ball and getting position on the 8-ball. So why try? If you make the 7-ball, it's next to impossible to play safe on the 8-ball. And by dislodging it from the cluster, you'll give your opponent a great opportunity to finish the game. Instead, play safe by pushing the 7-ball toward the corner pocket and drawing the cue ball back to the upper end of the table. Now the pressure is on your opponent. It will be very difficult for him to make a ball or play safe. In either case, he may do you a favor by bumping the 8-ball into the open. You would have to feel pretty good about your chances of winning.

Eight-Ball is more of a chess game than any other pool game. You have seven striped balls, and your opponent has seven solids. They're like opposing teams, and you should play accordingly. Use your team to your advantage. The position of your "players" can make his shots more difficult. "Snookering" your opponent is one of the most powerful safety plays in Eight-Ball. At the beginner level, Eight-Ball is not a run-out game. You will most likely get several turns at the table. Set yourself up, little by little, for opportunity to finish the game.

Which brings us to perhaps the most confusing part of Eight-Ball: how games are won and lost. It's my personal contention that you should have to win the game outright. You shouldn't let someone win it for you. *You* should have to pocket the 8-ball. The only way an opponent should be able to win the game for you is by pocketing the 8-ball in the wrong pocket or out of turn. On coin-operated tables, once the 8-ball goes into a pocket, you can't return it to the table. But the cue ball doesn't stay down, so if your opponent misses the 8-ball and scratches, you should get cue ball in hand. I don't like the idea of your winning the game if he scratches.

Requirements for winning the game also vary from location to location. Some house rules stipulate that you must sink the 8-ball in the same pocket in which you made the last ball of your group. Other rules say you must bank the 8-ball into a pocket in order to win. As I said before, make sure you and your opponent agree on all the rules before you break.

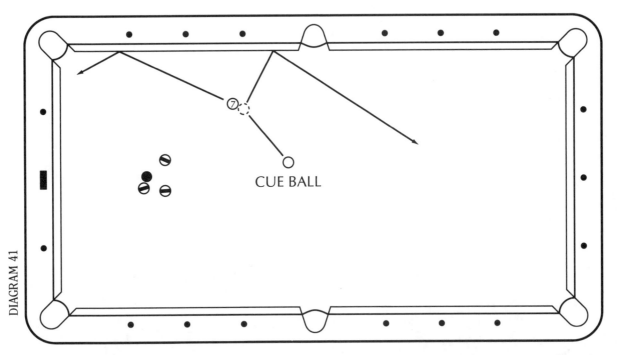

DIAGRAM 41

CUE BALL

Unless you have a chance to make the 8-ball, there's little sense in pocketing the last ball in your group—here, the 7-ball. Shoot it near, but not into, the corner pocket, and draw the cue ball up table. Leave that mess surrounding the 8-ball to your opponent. Odds are you'll be better off in the long run.

WHAT A DRAG!

One of the more interesting billiard legends concerns a woman player from Fort Wayne, Indiana, named Frances Anderson, who played in the early 1900s. As there were few, if any, women's tournaments in those days, most titles were self-proclaimed. Anderson claimed to be a champion and confidently offered $5,000 to any woman who could best her at pocket billiards.

Anderson toured the country, playing both women and men in exhibition matches. Early volumes of *Billiard Magazine* offer reports of Anderson's entertaining and well-received exhibitions. Legend states that for 25 years Anderson went undefeated against female challengers. She even proved victorious in roughly half of her matches against male opponents.

In the late twenties, Anderson performed exhibitions in Europe and received handsome sums for her appearances.

Appearances, though, can be deceiving! Apparently, Anderson later shocked the billiard world by announcing that her real name was Orie (of Newton, Kansas), not Frances, and that she was a he!

Now there's a case of miss-taken identity.

(courtesy of The Billiard Archive)

Billiard publications referred to Frances Anderson as "the clever woman pocket billiard player." If they only knew *how* clever "she" was!

(courtesy of The Billiard Archive)

The mysterious, silent Masked Marvel X was said to be adept at the game in either black or white dress— a true measure of a player's versatility!

Everyone needs a gimmick!

In the 1920s touring exhibition players were the rage. Naturally, competition in booking shows was fierce. Unless a player had the championship stature of a Willie Hoppe or Ralph Greenleaf, he or she needed a shtick!

No player of that period had a better routine than "Masked Marvel X." The mysterious marksman was equally adept at Balkline, Three-Cushion, and pocket billiards, and publicly offered to pay $10 to any player who defeated him in exhibition contests.

Not only did the masked man cover his face, he never spoke! He appeared for exhibition in full black dress, although, as his flyers stated, he wore "Full White Dress for Special Occasions." (Weddings, one would presume!)

As it turns out, Masked Marvel X was no fluke. Few reports from magazines of the day listed the mystifying artist on the losing side of the ledger.

In the standard Nine-Ball rack, the 1-ball must be at the top of the rack, with the 9-ball in the center. The remaining balls can be randomly racked.

9
Nine-Ball

While Straight Pool is the truest test of skill, and Eight-Ball is the most widely played game amongst beginners and amateurs, the game played most often in professional tournaments is Nine-Ball.

Nine-Ball is fast-paced and unpredictable, which makes it the most marketable pool game to mass audiences. It is easy to follow and features explosive break shots, spectacular shot making, and merciless safety play—all of which appeal to the American sports fan's seemingly insatiable appetite for action.

The appeal of Nine-Ball in recent years has been due to its action-packed nature. Straight Pool is thought to be too slow to hold a crowd's—or television audience's—attention. Eight-Ball has too many restrictions. Nine-Ball is cut-and-dried. Shoot the balls in rotation, first person to make the 9-ball wins. Anyone can play and/or follow that.

The game's pace and unpredictability also account for its long-standing reputation as a gambler's game. Games can be won on literally any shot—the break shot, the first shot of the game, the second shot, *any* shot. Because of that fact, a player with virtually no talent has a chance to beat a player of superior talent—especially in short matches.

I started playing Nine-Ball when I was a teenager, but there were never many Nine-Ball tournaments—a few here and there. By the mid-seventies, however, things began to change. Nine-Ball took off as a pro tournament game.

As you will come to see, luck plays a larger role in Nine-Ball than in any other pool game. Professional players have modified some of the rules to reduce the luck factor, but the game is still not for the faint of heart.

THE RULES

The object of Nine-Ball is to pocket the 9-ball, either on the break or any other legal shot.

Only the balls numbered 1 through 9 and the cue ball are used in Nine-Ball. The object balls are racked in a diamond shape, with the 1-ball on the foot spot and the 9-ball in the middle. The other seven balls may be placed in the rack at random.

THE OPENING BREAK

Since Nine-Ball is a rotation game, the cue ball must always strike the lowest-numbered ball on the table first. The break shot is no exception. From anywhere behind the head string, the cue ball must make contact with

Allen Hopkins is a great one-pocket player, as well as a champion in Nine-Ball and Straight Pool. Although he tends to "punch" at the ball, he's also managed to "punch out" his fair share of opponents.
(photo by Billie Billing)

Another tailor-made Nine-Ball player is David Howard. Possessor of one of the game's most powerful break shots, Howard jumps and dances when the balls are moving. He's probably pool's biggest user of body English!
(photo by Billie Billing)

the 1-ball first on the break shot. For a legal break, either a ball must be pocketed or at least four object balls must be driven to the rail. Barring a foul on the break, all pocketed balls count, and the player continues shooting.

If the shooter scratches on the break, all pocketed balls are spotted, and the incoming shooter has ball-in-hand behind the head string.

RULES OF PLAY

The cue ball must contact the lowest-numbered ball on the table first. To complete a legal shot, a ball must be pocketed or the cue ball or any object ball must contact the rail. Failure to do so is a foul. The incoming player has ball-in-hand anywhere on the table.

As long as the lowest-numbered ball is contacted first, any object balls that are pocketed count. Balls and intended pockets need not be declared. If the shooter scratches, balls pocketed on that shot are spotted, and the incoming shooter has ball-in-hand anywhere on the table. If the 9-ball is pocketed on any shot that meets the above requirements, the shooter wins the game.

Fouls on three consecutive shots result in a loss of game.

PUSH OUT

After the break shot, the player at the table (if a ball was pocketed, the breaker; if no balls were pocketed, the incoming player) has the option to "push out" or to shoot. A push-out is an illegal shot which merely entails pushing the cue ball to an alternate position on the table. The opponent may then choose to accept the table as is or force the first player to shoot again. The push shot after the break is not a foul. Any failure to make a legal hit following the push shot is a foul.

PLAYING NINE-BALL

Nine-Ball is a funny game. It shows no mercy and does not play favorites. Nine-Ball doesn't concern itself with how many balls you make. It only cares about *which* balls you make. I can break my neck running from the 1-ball through the 8-ball. But if I miss the 9-ball, and you successfully pocket it, you've won the game. Like life, Nine-Ball isn't always fair.

THE BREAK

The break in Nine-Ball is probably the biggest single advantage you can have in any pool game. It is all-important. You can lose a game of Nine-Ball without ever leaving your chair.

The Nine-Ball break is very important for more reasons than just giving you an opportunity to run out. On nearly every occasion, you can control the tempo of the game from the break. If you don't have a good shot at the 1-ball (or lowest-numbered ball if the 1-ball went in on the break shot), or you can see that attaining position on the 2-ball is going to be difficult, you can push out or play safe. You set the tone for the entire game when you break.

(courtesy of Carmine R. Manicone Photography)

Most beginners break with the cue ball near the head spot in Nine-Ball. No matter where you spot the cue ball, gauge your success over a handful of racks. If you're not having any luck pocketing balls on the break shot, remember: you're allowed to move your break position from rack to rack.

There is no magical position along the head string from which to break in Nine-Ball. During the course of a professional tournament match, in fact, you'll see the players move the cue ball along that line from one game to the next if they're failing to pocket a ball. When they find a spot that yields some success, they'll continue breaking from that spot.

Generally speaking, however, most players break from a point about halfway between the head spot and the side rail (Diagram 42). Breaking from this position tends to elicit greater response from the two balls which flank the 9-ball in a Nine-Ball rack. Those two balls move more than any other balls, which gives you a better chance of making a ball on the break.

These days, most pros break with the cue ball six to eight inches off the side rail. They feel that by breaking from the side they get more "action" out of the balls flanking the 9-ball.

The key to success on the Nine-Ball break is twofold. Obviously, you'd like to pocket a ball on the break shot to continue shooting. That's essential. But secondly, and just as importantly, you want to get a clear shot at the lowest-numbered ball on the table. A player who consistently makes a ball on the break and gets a decent shot at the lowest-numbered ball is going to be awfully tough to beat.

The main way to assure a decent shot at the lowest-numbered ball after the break is to keep the cue ball in the middle of the table. To do this on the break, hit the cue ball just above center. You don't want to draw the cue ball back up table, and you don't want too much follow, because the cue ball will follow into the area where the balls are bouncing off one another. A direct center ball hit is risky, too, because with no spin it's at the mercy of the object balls. A touch above center forces the ball to stay in the middle of the table.

Naturally, you have no control over other balls bumping into the cue ball. But you have a better chance of keeping the cue ball out of harm's way by bringing it back to the middle of the table.

When aiming the break shot, no matter where the cue ball is along the head string, aim directly through the 1-ball. This will transfer more direct impact on the rest of the balls. You usually sacrifice a little control for more power on the break. Those who can use power and retain control have a huge edge.

PUSHING OUT

The push shot after the break is an interesting facet of Nine-Ball. The push-out option was instituted to compensate for the luck factor on the break shot. (Because of the ball-in-hand–after-fouls rule, it didn't seem fair that a player could make four balls on the break, wind up "snookered" behind another ball, and have to shoot at the lowest-numbered ball. In fact, I once saw a player make seven balls on the break, and he wound up

(courtesy of Carmine R. Manicone Photography)

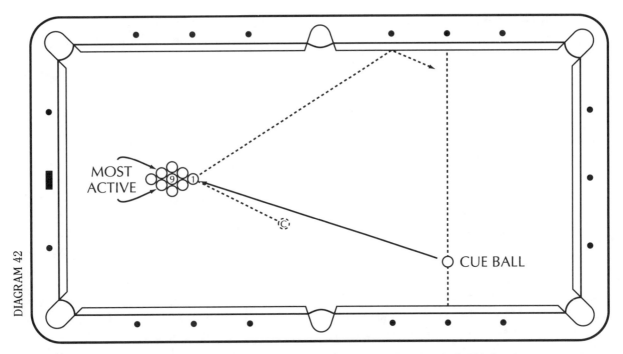

Most pros break from a point halfway between the head spot and side rail in Nine-Ball. This break causes maximum movement from the corner balls, which increases your chances of pocketing a ball.

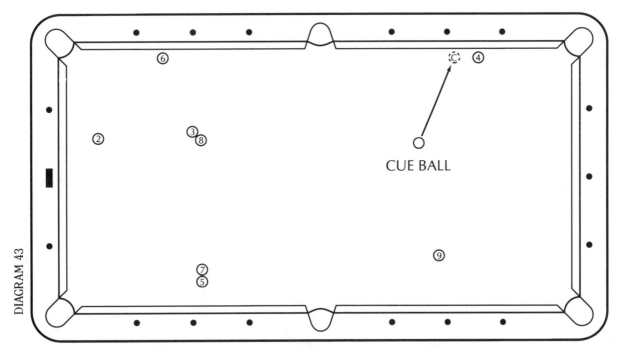

"Pushing out" after the break is an interesting cat-and-mouse game. Here, you're trying to lure your opponent into shooting at the 2-ball. Even if he makes the shot, he's got little chance of gaining position on the 3-ball.

stuck behind the 9-ball!) If you make a ball on the break but have no shot at the lowest-numbered ball, you can "push" the cue ball into a position which betters the chance of hitting that ball.

Your opponent has the option of accepting the table after your push shot, though, so you don't want to push the cue ball into too good a spot. That makes the push shot an interesting mind game. Take the situation illustrated in Diagram 43. You made the 1-ball on the break, but when the balls came to a halt, you were left with no shot on the 2-ball.

You might consider pushing to the side rail. On the surface, you're offering your opponent a tough, but tempting, shot to cut the 2-ball into pocket C. In reality, you're setting a trap. If he misses the 2-ball, you're back at the table. Even if he makes the 2-ball, he's not likely to gain position on the 3-ball (which is tied up with the 8-ball). In the event he opts to have *you* shoot, you could

try to play safe by banking the 2-ball back up table and sliding the cue ball in behind the 5-ball.

SAFETY PLAY

Years ago, we used to play "hit-the-ball," meaning the shooter had to make an honest attempt to hit the lowest-numbered ball. If the shooter failed to make contact, the incoming player had the option of shooting or making the initial player shoot again. A second consecutive miss would give the incoming player ball-in-hand anywhere on the table.

Today, however, the incoming player receives ball-in-hand on all fouls. That's an incredible advantage for a professional player. To that end, players in recent years have worked arduously on their safety games. If they can tie you up and get cue-ball-in-hand, rather than take a long, risky shot, it's to their advantage to do so.

Diagrams 45 and 46 depict a made-to-order safety situation. You really don't have a

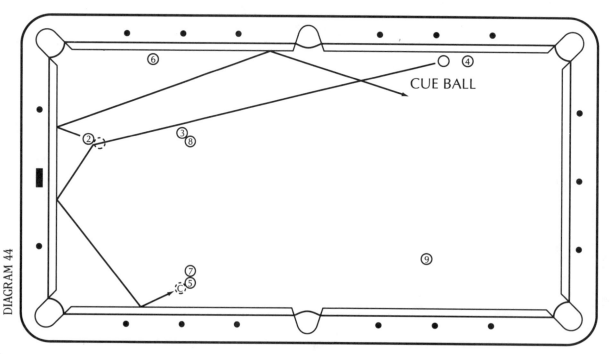

DIAGRAM 44

If your opponent makes you shoot again, your only hope is a safety on the 2-ball, hiding the cue ball behind the 5-ball and 7-ball.

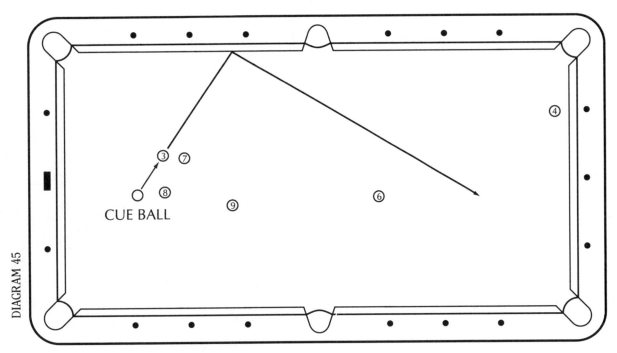

DIAGRAM 45

If you have a difficult shot and little chance of position on the next ball, play safe and put the onus on your opponent. A stop shot on the 3-ball will leave your opponent stuck behind the 7-ball.

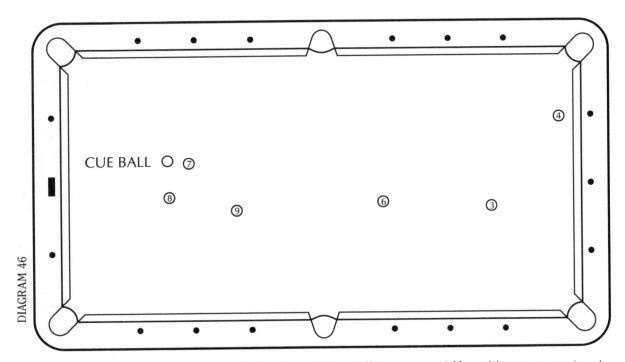

DIAGRAM 46

Not only has your safety tied up the cue ball, it also put the 3-ball in a more enviable position once you return to the table.

better than average chance of pocketing the 3-ball. One possibility is to bank it into the side pocket, but you'd be hard-pressed to gain position on the 4-ball.

Instead, simply punch the 3-ball off the side rail and up table. Don't worry about where the 3-ball stops. Just be sure to stop the cue ball in its tracks—right behind the 7-ball. You accomplish two things by playing safe. In all likelihood, you'll wind up with ball-in-hand. Also, the 3-ball is now in a spot from which position on the 4-ball is going to be easy. You'll be on your way!

STRATEGY

At the start, novices should work on running from one ball to the next. Learn to take care of the business at hand. Eventually you'll become more accustomed to looking beyond the next ball.

Remember, there are only nine balls on the entire table. Look at the layout and draw a plan of action. Don't play mindlessly into a trap from which there is no escape. If you fail to pocket the 9-ball, all the other balls you made amount to small consolation.

While you should always be aware of ways to end the game early—combinations and caroms into the 9-ball—don't spend the entire game firing wide-eyed at shortcuts. Learn to run nine balls. If a "dead" kiss or combination arises (such as the 9-ball dangling on the edge of a pocket, with the lowest-numbered ball a few inches away), take advantage. Otherwise, try to become a complete Nine-Ball player.

PRACTICE DRILLS

One of the best ways to learn how to think at the table is to watch other players, especially pros. Try to think with them as they circle the table. After they shoot, try to understand why they chose a particular shot.

Another way to develop knowledge of patterns is to practice the drill shown in Diagram 48. It's an offshoot of the two-ball run-

(courtesy of Carmine R. Manicone Photography)

How sweet it is! I've pocketed a ball on the break, I have an easy shot on the 1-ball in the side pocket, and the other object balls are out in the open. I'm out of here!

(courtesy of Carmine R. Manicone Photography)

Don't be overanxious! Before firing that 1-ball into the side pocket, notice that the 2-ball is tied to a nasty cluster along the side rail. Instead of making the 1-ball and risking a tough spot on the 2-ball, pass the problem off on your opponent.

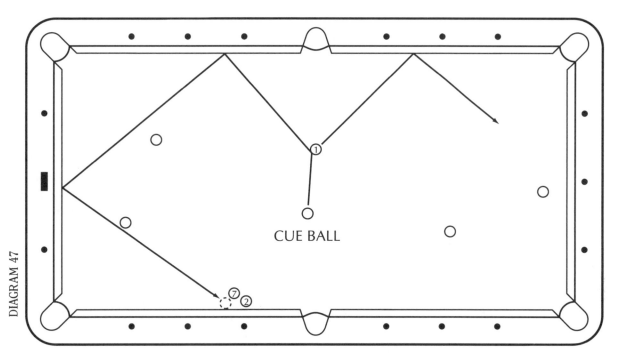

DIAGRAM 47

CUE BALL

The 1-ball looks easy enough, but if you look beyond the 1-ball, you'll see the 2-ball is tied up. Instead of making the 1-ball and risking a tough shot on the 2-ball, pass the problem to your opponent. Send the 1-ball up to the top of the table, and roll the cue ball two rails and in behind the 2-ball. Many times, a safety like that will win the game for you.

(courtesy of Carmine R. Manicone Photography)

You've chosen the correct option—a safety play. By sending the 1-ball to the top of the table, you've rolled the cue ball two rails and in behind the 2-ball. Many times, a safety play like that will win the game for you.

out drill described in Chapter 5, in the section on Position. Only this time, throw the 8-ball and 9-ball on the table and pocket them in rotation. Again, give yourself cue-ball-in-hand.

Here are a few important points to consider. Because you must sink the balls in rotation in Nine-Ball, it's usually important to have an angle on each shot. It's not uncommon in Nine-Ball to have to go to the other end of the table for your next shot. Straight-in shots make that a difficult task (although straight-in shots on the 9-ball are preferred). Don't try to be too perfect. Give yourself a general area or circle at which to aim. Few players can send a cue ball to an exact location. Pros play for zones which will keep their overall strategy intact.

Back to Diagram 48. With the 8-ball and 9-ball in place, set your cue ball for a slight angle on the 8-ball. A fairly delicate stroke, with a touch of draw, will allow the cue ball

to drift from the 8-ball into the optimum area (circle). What's left is a nice, short shot on the 9-ball to the side pocket.

Next, widen the distance between the 8-ball and 9-ball (Diagram 49). This makes your chore a bit more difficult. Again, a slight angle on the 8-ball will allow you to move the cue ball a greater distance. A little follow on the cue ball will send it off the end rail, to the side rail, and toward the bottom rail. Choose a path which gives you as large a position area as possible. In this case, once the cue ball passes the side pocket, the 9-ball becomes easier with every inch.

Once you've got the hang of this drill, add the 7-ball to the scenario—always running the balls in rotation. You'll quickly learn to appreciate the nuances of Nine-Ball—the fastest game on slate.

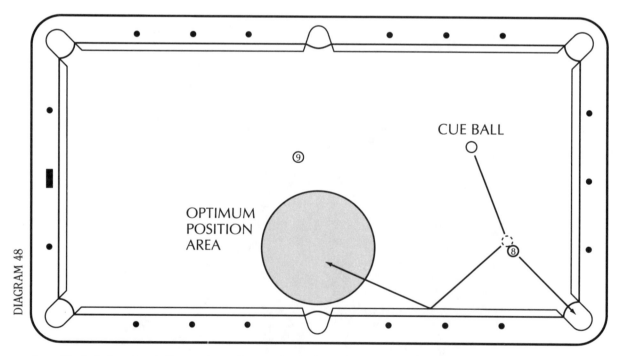

DIAGRAM 48

CUE BALL

⑨

OPTIMUM
POSITION
AREA

⑧

A terrific little learning drill is to throw the 8-ball and 9-ball out onto the table and give yourself ball-in-hand. Run the balls in rotation. Here, a slight angle on the 8-ball will provide an easy path to the 9-ball. Don't try to be perfect. You've got a large zone to work with for position on the 9-ball.

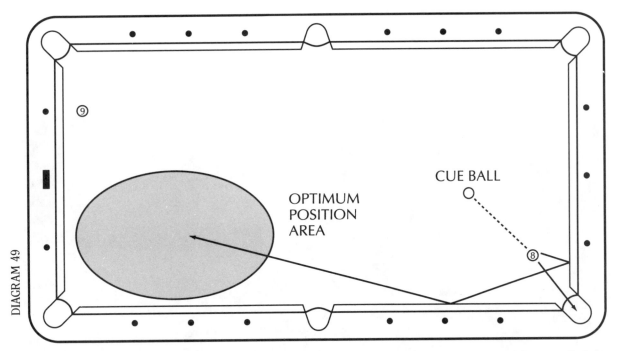

DIAGRAM 49

Even though the 8-ball and 9-ball are at opposite ends of the table, a modest angle and a little follow are all that's needed to get the cue ball traveling on a perfect path toward the 9-ball. If the cue ball stops anywhere in the circle, you'll have a decent shot on the 9-ball.

⛧ JOHN KNOWS BILLIARDS ⛧

Two-sport star Bo Jackson has nothing on the late, great Johnny Kling!

A native of Kansas City, Missouri, Kling was a standout catcher for the Chicago Cubs at the turn of the century. Contract disputes were prevalent even in 1909, and Kling shocked the baseball world by sitting out one entire season.

What did he do with his spare time? Kling displayed his incredible versatility by besting Charles "Cowboy" Weston to win the 1909 World Pocket Billiards Championship!

Kling returned to baseball in 1910 and played on the Cub squads that featured the "Tinkers-to-Evers-to-Chance" infield trio. Later, Kling and pocket billiard champion Bennie Allen opened the famous and highly successful Kling-Allen Bowling Alley and Billiard Parlour in Kansas City.

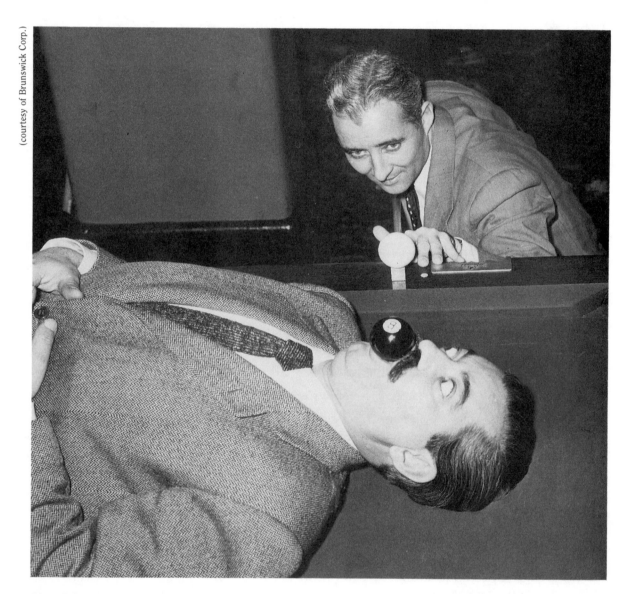

Jerry Colonna, radio, stage, and screen luminary of the fifties, is behind the 8-ball (literally!) as a human target for pocket billiard champion Willie Mosconi.

10
Trick Shots

All professional pool players love exhibition work. For one, it's a player's chance to turn entertainer—tell a few jokes, make a few balls. Also, it's guaranteed money. You don't have to worry about finishing fifth, sixth, or last, like you do at tournaments. Exhibitions are like going to a tournament and knowing you're going to finish first!

The catch is, not all players put on good exhibitions. Exhibition play really is an art, and some players simply lack the showmanship and patter required to keep an audience entertained. During the mid-eighties, I was working between 50 and 100 days of shows each year as a Lite Beer All Star. Two or three shows a day—believe me, that can be grueling work!

The toughest part of exhibition work is holding a crowd's attention and keeping them amused ·when your shots aren't falling. It's like the old stand-up comic's credo: don't let them see you sweat.

What makes exhibition play so exciting for audiences is the opportunity to see the best players in the business show you feats of amazing skill—with a little chicanery thrown in.

Naturally, the most popular and intriguing part of a pocket billiard exhibition is the dazzling array of trick and fancy shots the performing pro unleashes on the crowd. In the old days, the highlight of an exhibition was the player's attempt at a long run. Since championship tournament matches end at a predetermined number of points, most of the longest runs ever recorded took place in an exhibition setting. My personal high run is 321, established during an exhibition. The longest pocket billiard run in history (as recognized by the Billiard Congress of America) is Willie Mosconi's famed 526, which he accomplished during an exhibition match in Springfield, Ohio, in 1954.

While some of the game's great players have excelled at exhibition play as well as tournament competition (Mosconi, Jimmy Caras, Lou Butera, and Ralph Greenleaf immediately come to mind), some of the world's greatest trick-shot artists are players who enjoyed little success in professional tournaments. In fact, they specialize almost exclusively as exhibition players. Willie Jopling, Tom Rossman, and Paul Gerni are such players. Mike Massey, called "Tennessee Tarzan" because of his amazing strength, is a solid pro but a phenomenal exhibition talent.

As most players are quick to point out, the shots performed during an exhibition can be divided into two categories: trick shots and skill shots. Trick shots are generally consid-

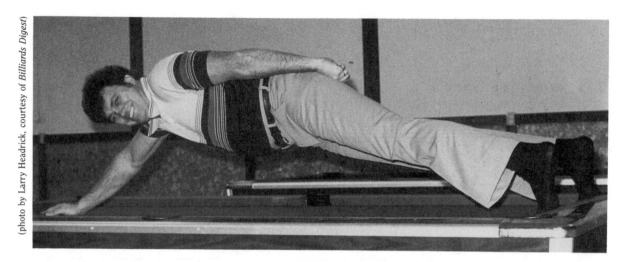

(photo by Larry Headrick, courtesy of *Billiards Digest*)

They don't call Mike Massey "Tennessee Tarzan" for nothing! His Finger Pool shots are a wonder to behold. Here, Mike gets a little exercise by doing one-arm pushups in his family rec room.

ered those shots whose success lies strictly in how they are set up. If they are set up properly, they can be executed by virtually anyone. They're ball-reaction shots.

Skill shots, also called *fancy shots* or *stroke shots* in some circles, are shots which require raw pool talent. It may be in the form of excessive draw, a jump shot, a masse shot (curving the cue ball by striking down on the edge of the ball from a steep angle), or a shot which requires extreme English. As in most sports, some players execute certain shots better than others. Massey has an incredibly powerful stroke, and his exhibition reflects this talent. A Mike Massey show is sure to feature stroke shots that other pros simply can't pull off. These are not shots you can set up and teach a beginner.

Another pro, Sammy Jones, jumps the cue ball over object balls (and other obstructions) with mind-boggling accuracy. When Sammy puts on a performance, an air traffic controller is usually brought in to make sure the air lanes are clear. (It's best not to sit in the front row at such an exhibition!)

The shots described in this chapter are trick shots. Some will require you to impart a little English onto the cue ball but, for the most part, the trick is in setting the shot properly.

Don't assume, however, that trick shots are easy. The setup has to be perfect, and proper speed and aim come into play on most of the shots. Also, all tables play differently. Variances in cushion rubber, cloth, humidity, etc., cause different reactions. Some tables play long, meaning balls tend to carom on a wider angle. Other tables play short. Adjustments need to be made when setting up shots to compensate for the variances. All exhibition players try some standard shots well before showtime so they can get acquainted with the table's tendencies.

When you try these shots at home or at the local billiard room, don't get frustrated if they don't work perfectly on the first attempt. Trick shots, like any other shots, take practice. Watch to see which balls are missing the pockets, and make adjustments. Also—and this is a key point in any trick shot—be sure the balls are frozen. Most trick shots rely on dead kisses and combinations. The balls must be frozen, either to the rail or other balls.

If the balls don't seem to stay frozen, here's a little trick—although your local poolroom owner may not be thrilled to see you do this. Grab a spare ball and gently tap the top of the ball you're trying to keep in place. It makes a slight indentation in the cloth, which keeps the ball from rolling.

In the accompanying diagrams, the dotted lines indicate lines of aim when setting up the shot. Solid lines show the ball's actual path when the shot is executed.

❦ UNUSUAL TRICK SHOTS ❧

Trick shots have been around a long time. Some historians have traced trick shots back to the late 1700s.

Generally speaking, trick shots are, in and of themselves, unusual. But as the saying goes, "You ain't seen nothin' yet!"

Quite a few trick shots require some kind of aid or prop—a paper bag, a handkerchief, penny wrappers, cubes of chalk, and even human assistants. I've performed a lot of trick shots in my day, all over the world. In all of my shots, I try to keep one thing constant: I use my cue stick.

That may seem relatively obvious, but trick shots made by propelling the cue ball with something other than a cue stick do exist. Some of them, in fact, are downright incredible.

Mike Massey, a fellow professional, plays "Finger Pool." A man with exceptionally strong hands, "Tennessee Tarzan," as he is known, squirts the cue ball as if he were snapping his fingers. Because of his strength, Massey is able to apply incredible extremes of English and draw on the cue ball—far more than is possible with a cue tip.

Massey didn't invent Finger Pool—players have been flicking the cue ball with their fingers since the early 1800s—but Massey may well have perfected it. "Cue Ball Kelly" was another expert at Finger Pool.

Another tricky way to pocket balls has been perfected by guys who just can't resist shooting off their mouths. That's right! A few people have actually learned how

(photos by Billie Billing)

Well, blow me down! The shots that Steve Simpson can make by shooting the cue ball out of his mouth are truly amazing.

Trick shot artist Professor Lewis, who toured in the early 1920s, was noted for his *nose* shots.

to shoot a cue ball from their mouths with amazing accuracy. I've seen players like George Middleditch of Michigan and Steve Simpson of Tennessee make "spot shots" and three-rail kick shots by spitting the cue ball onto the table. And I don't mean dribbling the cue ball out onto the table; these guys can really fire the ball!

Believe it or not, I cannot fit (nor do I wish to fit) a cue ball in my mouth.

Not that I look upon these trick shot artists with my nose in the air. In fact, there have been a few players who specialized in pocketing balls with their noses! The most noted of these nasal sharpshooters was Professor Henry Lewis, a noted billiards player who performed exhibitions in the 1920s. Aiming out of the corner of one eye, Professor Lewis would propel the ball with the side of his nose—sort of a low-profile golf putt!

Incredibly, Professor Lewis once recorded a run of 46 consecutive balls! You might say the professor had a nose for accuracy.

1. HIT AND RUN

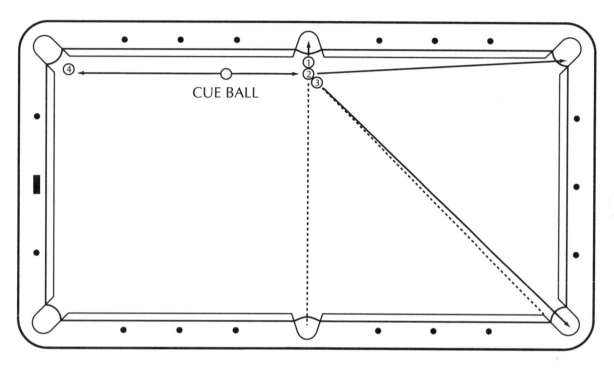

CUE BALL

Here's a fairly easy shot that allows you to show off your newfound ability to draw the cue ball.

To Set Up: Place the cue ball several inches off the side rail near the third diamond. Lodge the 4-ball in the jaws of the lower left corner pocket.

Place the 1-ball an inch or so out from the left side pocket. Freeze the 2-ball to the 1-ball, aimed directly to the opposite side pocket. The 3-ball should be frozen to the 2-ball, aimed to the right tip of the top right corner pocket.

To Execute: Strike the cue ball well below center, hitting the 2-ball flush. The 1-ball will dive into the nearest pocket (the side), while the 2-ball rifles up table to the left corner pocket. The 3-ball will head directly to the upper right corner. Finally, with proper draw, the cue ball will scoot back down to the corner to bump the 4-ball into the pocket.

If, say, the 3-ball misses the corner pocket, simply adjust the line of aim slightly. If your cue ball misses the 4-ball or hits the long rail on its way back to the corner, move it an inch or so left or right.

2. BROKEN PYRAMID

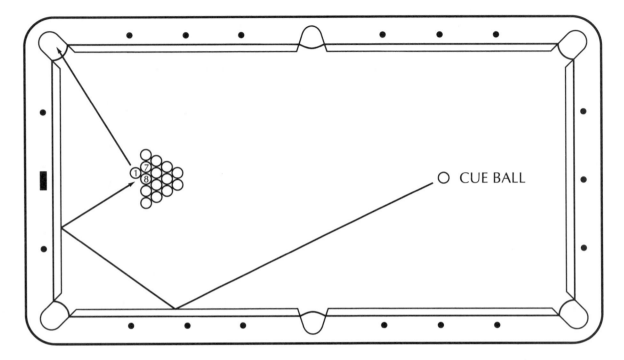

Although this shot is not likely to come up in a Straight Pool game, if it ever did, you would be ready!

Say your opponent missed his break shot but left you in a precarious position. The cue ball is resting on the head spot, and the 1-ball is tucked neatly behind the rack, frozen to the 7-ball and 8-ball. Imagine his surprise when you call the 1-ball in the corner pocket!

To Set Up: Rack all 15 balls in the triangle at the foot spot. Remove the apex ball and place it, as shown, below the rack.

To Execute: This shot requires some right English, a touch above center. Aim the cue ball to hit the long rail near the second diamond. It should carom to the end rail, between the first and second diamonds, and up to the inside portion of the 1-ball. As long as you don't hit the 1-ball flush or on the outside edge, the 1-ball should scoot cleanly to the corner pocket.

Before you bother setting up all 15 object balls, practice your carom off the rails to establish the proper aim and English. Continually re-racking the object balls while you practice this shot can get to be a pain!

3. CHAIN REACTION

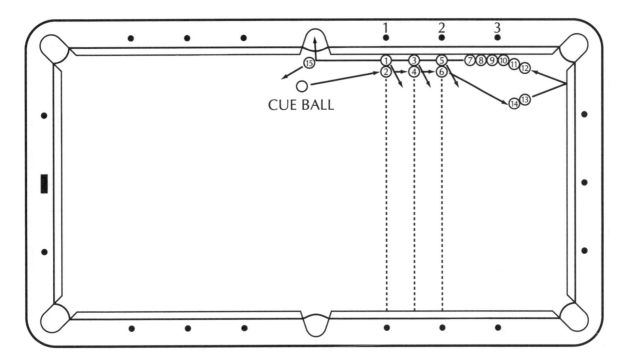

This is truly a shot in which proper setup is the key. Set up correctly, all you need to do is hit the first ball and get out of the way!

To Set Up: The easiest ball to set up is the 15-ball, which sits several inches out from the side pocket. Freeze the 1-ball to the long rail at the first diamond. Freeze the 2-ball to the 1-ball, on an angle just above the diamond along the opposite rail. Do the same with the 3-ball and 4-ball halfway between the first and second diamonds. At the second diamond, freeze the 5-ball and 6-ball, again on a slight angle. (There must be room for the ball frozen to the rail to escape.)

Between the second and third diamonds, freeze the 7-ball to the rail. The 8-ball, 9-ball, and 10-ball should be frozen directly behind the 7-ball. The 11-ball and 12-ball should be frozen to the 10-ball, on an angle to the bottom rail between the pocket and the fourth diamond. The 13-ball and 14-ball should be approximately 10 inches from the side rail,

frozen on a slight angle to the bottom rail. Finally, place the cue ball a foot or so from the side rail, near the 15-ball.

To Execute: In case you're wondering, the object is to pocket the 7-ball in the side pocket! You accomplish this by striking the 2-ball, forcing it into the 4-ball. Thus starts the chain reaction. The 4-ball strikes the 6-ball, which shoots down toward the 14-ball. The 14-ball pushes the 13-ball to the bottom rail and back up to the 12-ball. The frozen combination of balls 12, 11, 10, 9, and 8 causes the 7-ball to ride the rail toward the side pocket. The 7-ball bumps into the 15-ball and drops harmlessly into the side pocket.

The key points of contact in this shot are between the 6-ball and 14-ball, and between the 13-ball and 12-ball. As long as the 6-ball hits the 14-ball, and the 13-ball bumps the 12-ball, the rest of the chain reaction is pretty natural.

4. GET THE POINT?

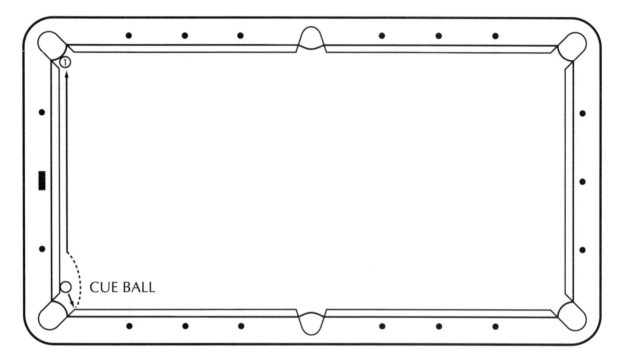

CUE BALL

Everyone likes a shot that makes him feel like he's doing something very intricate.

On this shot, you'll use nothing more than a center ball hit, with moderate speed. Simple as can be. Yet the cue ball will be launched into the air, after which it will fly to the opposite corner of the table to pocket an object ball!

To Set Up: Place the 1-ball at the edge of the left corner pocket, and the cue ball along the bottom rail just short of the point.

To Execute: Aim the cue ball for the opposite point of the corner pocket, and use a moderate stroke. The cue ball will contact the point of the rail, which will send it into the air and toward the opposite corner pocket. It will bounce several times on the table and bump the 1-ball into the pocket.

This shot may take some practice to achieve the proper angle to the 1-ball, but getting the cue ball up off the table should be easy to master.

GETTING YOUR MONEY'S WORTH

Some trick-shot shows can prove disappointing, but few crowds lucky enough to have witnessed a performance by Charles Peterson in the 1920s and 1930s ever went away dissatisfied.

A tireless promoter of the game, Peterson eschewed competition to bring billiards to high schools and colleges across the country. Peterson was also a phenomenal trick-shot artist, inventing many trick shots still used today and perfecting a few that have rarely been duplicated successfully.

(courtesy of *Billiards Digest*)

A tireless promoter of billiards, Charlie Peterson was also one of the finest trick-shot artists ever.

One such shot featured a half-dollar piece standing upright between two object balls near the foot-spot. Using a normal billiard cue, Peterson could send the half-dollar rolling to the head rail, where it banked back toward and *through* the two balls!

Had Peterson's incredible coin shot not been captured on various film shorts, few people born after Peterson's death in 1962 would believe the shot was possible.

5. THE BUTTERFLY

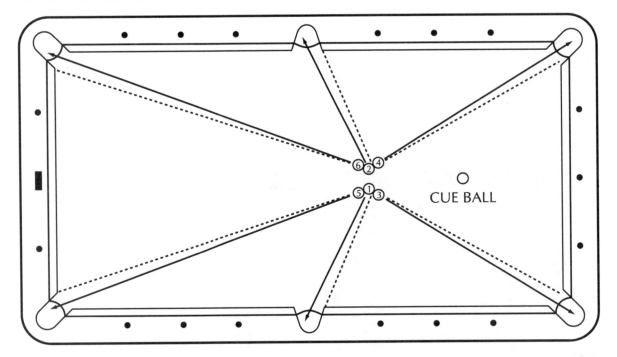

Everyone appreciates the beauty of a butterfly, and this shot is no exception. It's often performed in trick-shot shows and is so easy to execute that most performers ask a child to hit the cue ball. As long as the cue ball is aimed through the center of the opening, the object balls will obey like Marines.

To Set Up: Place the 1-ball and 2-ball slightly less than a full ball's width apart. The 3-ball and 4-ball (which should be even with the first diamond beneath the side pocket) should be frozen to the 1-ball and 2-ball. Their lines of aim should be to the inside edge of the corner pockets. The line between the 1-ball and 3-ball should run to the bottom edge of the side pocket. A similar line should cut between the 2-ball and 4-ball to the opposite side pocket.

Freeze the 5-ball to the 1-ball, on a line to the head rail, just shy of the corner pocket. The 6-ball should be frozen to the 2-ball, in line with the head rail an inch or so short of the opposite corner pocket.

To Execute: When these balls are frozen and lined up correctly, simply drive the cue ball between the 1-ball and 2-ball. Once the cue ball contacts the 1-ball and 2-ball simultaneously, you'll pocket six balls in six different pockets!

6. WILLIAM TELL HAD IT EASY!

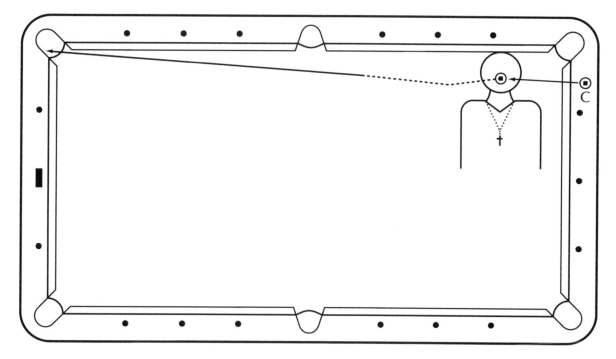

Shooting an apple off someone's head is child's play compared to shooting a pool ball out of someone's mouth!

Realistically, the toughest part of this shot is convincing someone to be your "volunteer"—especially when you tell the audience you've never attempted this shot before!

To Set Up: Have your volunteer lie across one end of the table, his head flat on the cloth and just short of the side rail. Place a piece of chalk between his teeth, and instruct him to clench his teeth together to hold the chalk in place. Next, rest a pool ball on the piece of chalk. (A new piece of chalk, which has a perfectly curved groove, works best for holding the ball in place.)

At this point, I normally drop a flower across the volunteer's (or is that *victim's?*) chest.

Stack two pieces of chalk on the rail, and place the cue ball atop the second piece. Aim to pocket the object ball in the upper corner pocket.

To Execute: Drop to one knee and shoot the cue ball up at the object ball. The object ball will zip up the table and, hopefully, into the corner pocket. The cue ball will fall harmlessly down onto the table.

I suggest practicing this shot by resting the object ball at the top of a plastic bottle before you try it out on any of your friends.

7. EASY AS 1-2-3

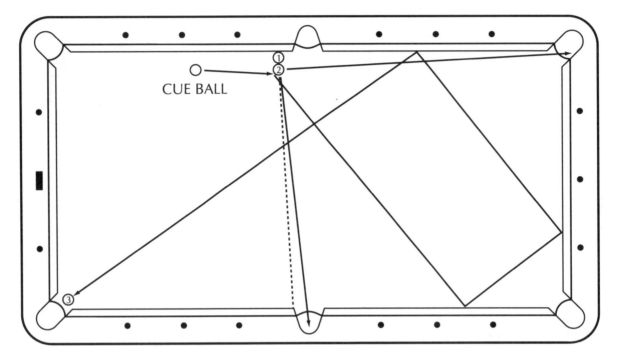

CUE BALL

Hundreds of trick-shot variations (including my Lite Beer shot!) are built from this simple foundation.

To Set Up: Place the 3-ball at the edge of the lower right corner pocket. Freeze the 1-ball to the side rail, about an inch below the side pocket. Freeze the 2-ball to the 1-ball, aimed directly across the table to the opposite side rail. Place the cue ball about a ball's width from the side rail, even with the second diamond below the side pocket.

To Execute: The shot will require some left English, and the cue ball should be hit above center. Aim to hit about less than half of the 2-ball. The 2-ball will race up to the left corner pocket, while the 1-ball caroms across the table to the opposite side pocket. The cue ball, carried by its left English, spins off three rails and down to the corner pocket, where it pockets the 3-ball.

GIVE THAT MAN A HAND!

You've got to hand it to Harvey Hendrickson. The Jamestown, New York, native probably made more money on limited billiard skills than anyone in the history of the game, save for "Minnesota Fats."

Hendrickson toured the country and astounded crowds everywhere by being able to pick up (with one hand) and hold 15 balls in the same hand!

Some people tend to take their games a bit too seriously. Mary, Queen of Scots, was one such sports junkie.

Besides being a certified billiard nut, Mary Stuart was an avid golfer. So avid, in fact, that she was accused of playing a round or two only days after her husband's death in 1563.

Her billiard habits were no less intense. After being imprisoned in 1587 for plotting the assassination of her cousin, Queen Elizabeth, Mary spent her time awaiting execution by playing billiards. When her table was taken from her on the eve of her date with the axman, she is said to have complained to the archbishop. (Cruel and unusual punishment, no doubt, was her charge.)

Legend also has it that, after being cut down to size, Mary's body was wrapped in the cloth from her billiard table!

(courtesy of The Billiard Archive)

Harvey Hendrickson made a living off of his ability to hold 15 balls in one hand.

8. ONCE AROUND THE TABLE, AND HOME

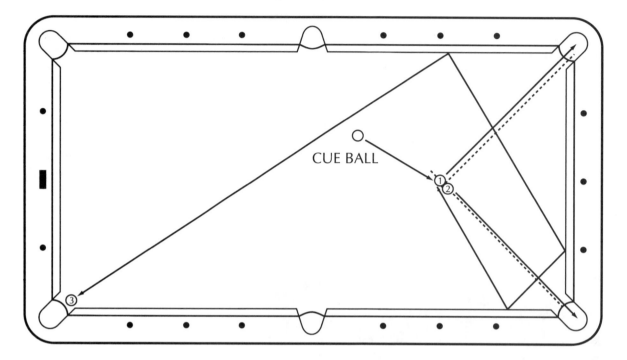

CUE BALL

Here's an opportunity to put your kiss-shot knowledge to practical use.

To Set Up: Place the 1-ball on the head spot. Freeze the 2-ball to the 1-ball in such a manner that the 2-ball is a dead kiss to one corner pocket, while the 1-ball is a dead kiss to the opposite corner. As explained in Chapter 5, a line between two frozen balls, perpendicular to a line running through the centers of the balls, will show the path along which the first ball will travel. As long as the cue ball hits the high side of the 1-ball, the 1-ball and 2-ball will shoot into the opposite corner pockets.

To Execute: Now all that's left is to figure the proper angle from which the cue ball will travel three rails and into the 3-ball. I suggest placing the cue ball just above the side pocket, between the center of the table and the side rail. Since pinpoint aim on the 1-ball is not crucial, don't be afraid to use a little left English. This will spin the cue ball around the table. Whatever adjustments are needed should be on the cue ball only.

A little practice to gain the right angle, and this shot will be easy.

9. PHOTO FINISH

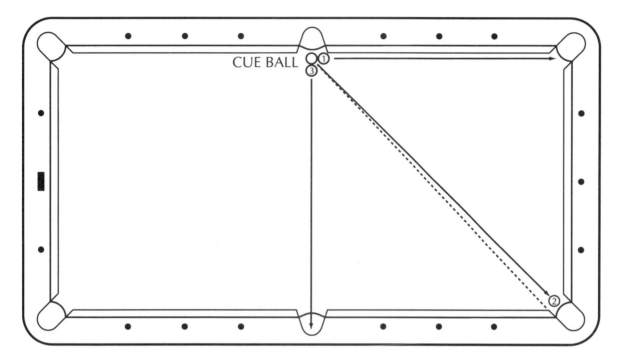

Which ball goes into a pocket first? If you can figure that out, let me know. They should all go in simultaneously.

To Set Up: Place the 2-ball in the jaws of the right corner pocket. The cue ball should be situated an inch or two out from the side pocket. Freeze the 1-ball to the cue ball, lined up with the upper left corner pocket. The 3-ball should also be frozen to the cue ball, aimed directly across to the opposite side pocket. (The 1-ball, cue ball, and 3-ball should form a perfect right angle.)

To Execute: Simply aim the cue ball at the lower tip of the right corner pocket. The 1-ball will go to the left corner pocket, the 3-ball will zip across to the side, and the cue ball will hit the 2-ball head-on.

10. LAZY MAN'S RACK

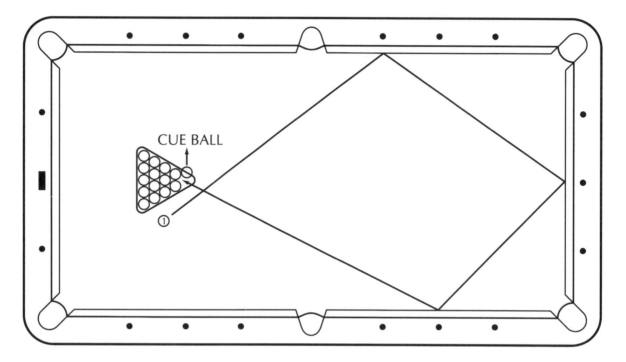

An old dog that many exhibition players use as an opener, this shot is still a staple of Mosconi's exhibitions.

To Set Up: Rack all 15 balls in the triangle at the foot spot. Remove the apex ball (in this case the 1-ball), but leave the rack in place. Lift the front of the rack and let it rest on the cue ball, which you've placed directly above the first ball of the second row.

To Execute: From the other side of the rack, aim the 1-ball, with just a touch of right English, for the first diamond above the side pocket. The 1-ball should carom to the middle of the head rail, over to approximately the middle of the side rail, and into the vacancy at the front of the rack. When it reaches the front of the rack, the 1-ball will kiss the cue ball away, and the triangle will fall back into place.

Now you're ready to start your game!

MIZERAK LITE BEER COMMERCIAL

It doesn't seem possible that more than 10 years have gone by since I taped my first Lite Beer commercial! I always refer to it as the 30 seconds that changed my life, and believe me, it did change my life forever!

At the time, I was a part-time pool player and full-time grammar school teacher. I was also on the board of directors of the Professional Pool Players Association, or PPPA, which I helped form in 1976. A large New York City–based advertising agency, then called Backer & Spielvogel, had developed a wonderfully original series of commercials for Miller Brewing Company's new Lite Beer brand. The commercials centered around not-so-famous ex-jocks. I think New York Jets fullback Matt Snell was the first ever Lite Beer All Star.

Anyway, the agency contacted our PPPA office. They wanted four pool players to audition for a beer commercial. It seemed logical that four of the original PPPA founders should get a shot at the spot, so we selected then-PPPA president Ray Martin, Pete Margo, Allen Hopkins, and me for the tryout.

Needless to say, I was a nervous wreck before the audition—and with good reason. Somehow or other, I never received a copy of the script! The first time I saw it was when I was sitting in the waiting room before the audition. Luckily, I was the last of the four players to be tested. I did notice that the other four players were in and out in about a half-hour. I was in that studio for four hours! I went home and told my wife, Karen, that there was no possible way I was going to get that job. The whole day went by like a blur.

Incredibly, the following day Marty Blackman, Miller's agent for the Lite Beer All Stars, called me and said, "Steve, you've got it." I couldn't believe it.

I literally danced around the living room!

About a month later, we shot the actual commercial at the Knickerbocker Bar & Grill in New York. It was one of the longest, yet most enjoyable, days of my life. The commercial entailed completing three or four separate trick shots while simultaneously reciting the script. The timing had to be just perfect.

Well, I managed to knock over the glass of beer on the table twice, ruining the cloth. Then there were times when the lighting wasn't just right or the lines got jumbled. In all, the commercial took an amazing 191 takes. Luckily, the cue ball never hit the Lite Beer bottle that was near the corner pocket. That bottle was hand-painted for the commercial and cost over $200. Now that's an expensive bottle of beer!

THE LITE BEER SHOT(S)

No matter where I go, I'm expected to perform the shot I used in the Miller Lite Beer commercial. Seeing as how that shot changed my entire life—for the better!—I'm always happy to accommodate.

The fact is, that commercial actually consisted of a sequence of three trick shots. Not only did I have to execute each trick shot, but I had to be in position for the next shot.

Few beginners will be able to complete this shot, but I'd like to include it anyway—even though you might think I'm just showin' off.

Part I is a dead kiss/dead combination shot using the 7-ball and 8-ball (see Trick Shot Number 8). Freeze the 7-ball and 8-ball, with the 8-ball aimed at the corner pocket. The balls should be just far enough off the rail so the 7-ball is a kiss to the near corner. What made this shot so tough was having to hit rail-first, with draw, to keep the cue ball in position for the second shot. You don't

have to hit this shot very hard.

Part II is a dead combination, with the 1-ball frozen to the 9-ball and aimed directly to the far corner pocket. The shot is relatively easy but, again, rolling the cue ball into position for the grand finale is not. Contact the 9-ball, which is at the edge of the side pocket, with high left English. Not much power is needed here, either. The 9-ball will drop into the side pocket, and the 10-ball will scoot to the corner. The cue ball should drift to within 6 inches of the middle diamond on the long rail for position on the six-ball combination.

Part III is difficult to set up. The 2-ball is frozen to the rail, just beneath the point on the side pocket. The 1-ball is frozen to the 2-ball, aiming straight across the table. The 5-ball and 4-ball are frozen near the top half of the same side pocket, a little farther out than the 2-1 combination. They should be aimed toward the point on the opposite side pocket. Freeze the 3-ball to the 4-ball, in a line just shy of the corner pocket. Set the 6-ball as shown.

Hopefully, you've left the cue ball in line

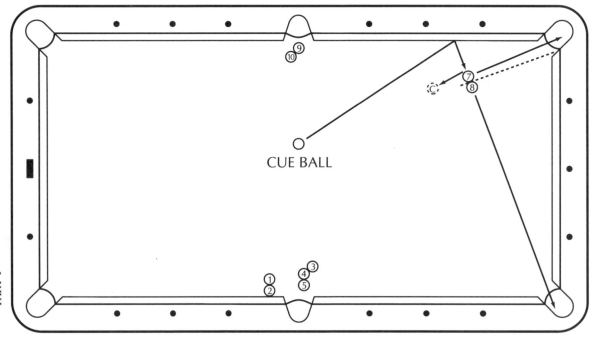

with the 1-ball. Stroke it with high left English. The 2-ball will go cross-side, the 1-ball will carom off the 4-ball and into the side, and the 5-ball will drop in the same side pocket. The 4-ball will run into the corner pocket, and the 3-ball will angle to the opposite corner pocket. The cue ball will run three rails to make the 6-ball.

That's it! Ten balls with three shots. And don't forget to lift the bottle of Lite Beer before the cue ball reaches the 6-ball!

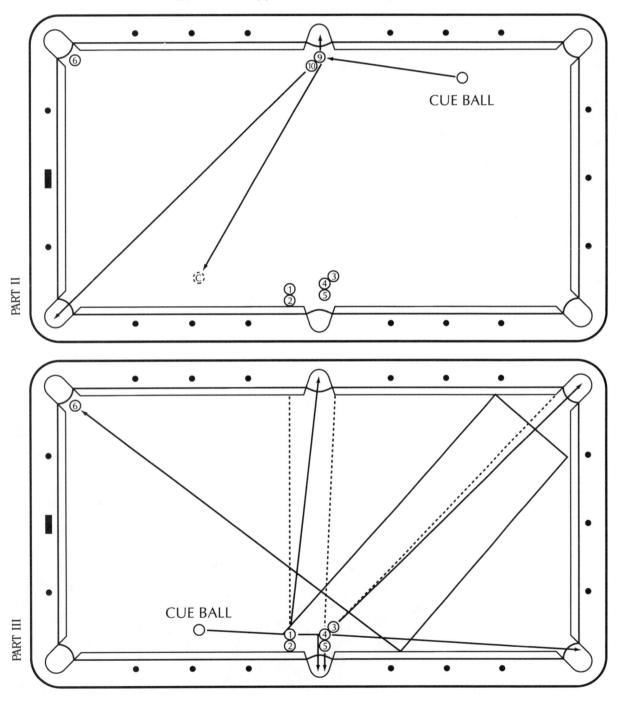

PART II

CUE BALL

PART III

CUE BALL

Thirty seconds that changed my life. This was taken during a break in filming the Lite Beer "Just Showin' Off" commercial at the Knickerbocker Bar & Grill in New York City. After 191 takes, the balls had all but worn a path to the pockets!
(courtesy of Steve Mizerak)

Here's the full setup for my Lite Beer shot. When executed properly, the shots take 23 seconds. I set this shot up 191 times while filming the commercial!
(courtesy of Carmine R. Manicone Photography)

11
Home Is Where the Pool Table Is

Once you've been smitten by the beauty and mystery of pocket billiards, occasional trips to the neighborhood nouveau pool rooms simply won't be enough. The pool rooms are great— you were introduced to the game there, made new friends there, and enjoy the social atmosphere the rooms offer. But you want more.

Invariably, while lounging in your den watching a pool tournament on ESPN (of course you've got cable), you'll find yourself sizing up rooms in the house, trying to figure where a pool table will fit. Really, no home should be without a "parlor" devoted to pool. Think of all the entertaining you can do and

what a hit your parties will be. Besides, with a home room, you'll be able to improve your game to a level you never dreamed was possible.

And if your home happens to be a four-room condominium in a 45-story downtown high rise, don't be discouraged. The options are virtually endless. For starters, how about a convertible dining room table/pool table? After a wonderful dinner, just pop off the tabletop and rack up a game of Eight-Ball. (Remember the Clampetts' "fancy eatin' table" in "The Beverly Hillbillies"?)

The key to setting up a home billiard

(courtesy of *Billiards Digest*)

Even if you have the space, don't think you're obligated to fill every inch of it!

room is suiting the table to the room's dimensions. In other words, don't try to jam a 6-by-12-foot Snooker table into a room that measures 8-by-14-feet. The table may fit physically, but the game itself will be reduced to something akin to Arena Football.

When determining what size table will fit in the room you've designated the pool room, remember that the average cue length is 57 inches (4 feet, 9 inches). Therefore, if you allow for, say, 5 feet from each rail to the nearest wall (or breakable object), you'll have room to execute any shot on the table. (Taking into account your normal backswing, you'll need the entire 5 feet when the cue ball is frozen to one of the cushions.)

As was mentioned earlier, the standard dimensions of pool tables are 5-by-10-foot, 4½-by-9-foot, 4-by-8-foot, 3½-by-7-foot, and,

occasionally, 3-by-6-foot. Table measurements are usually referred to by the approximate length of the table, since all tables are twice as long as they are wide. In other words, it's appropriate to refer to a 4½-by-9-foot table as a 9-footer. Reference to table sizes in this manner is yet another step toward gaining acceptance as a pool aficionado.

The chart on the opposite page gives optimum room dimensions for various table sizes. Obviously, there are ways to compensate for slightly smaller rooms. The easiest way to deal with a lack of elbow room is to have a short cue on hand. Most cue manufacturers either already make, or have the ability to make, cues that measure 45–50 inches. (If you're *really* cramped for space, try unscrewing your cue and using only the shaft to execute the shot!)

Table Size (Width × Length)	Optimum Room Width	Optimum Room Length
3′ × 6′	12′-13′	15′-16′
3½′ × 7′	12½′-13½′	16′-17′
4′ × 8′*	13′-14′	17′-18′
4½′ × 9′	13½′-14½′	18′-19′
5′ × 10′	14′-15′	19′-20′
6′ × 12′	(plan on parking the cars outside!)	

*8-foot tables come in two sizes: the "home 8-foot" actually measures 44″ × 88″, while the "pro 8-foot" measures 48″ × 96″.

(courtesy of *Billiards Digest*)

(courtesy of Brunswick Billiards Corp.)

When buying a home table from a reliable billiard dealer, you'll likely be given a half dozen or so one-piece maple cues, a triangle (plastic rack), a full set of balls (cue ball and 15 numbered balls), a bridge, a light plastic table cover, and a brush to keep the cloth clean.

In some cases, oftentimes depending on the quality (or price) of the table, the billiard dealer will include a cue rack to store your cue sticks, and a rack for the balls. (These may be combined as one unit.)

But decorating your own home billiard room doesn't stop there. Not by a long shot. For starters, you may decide to eschew the "standard" accessories package for higher-end items. For instance, a nice solid oak triangle ($30–$70) may be more suited to your very discriminating taste. A matching oak wall rack ($200–$500) would certainly look nice in your finished basement. Perhaps a wall rack with a frosted oval mirror and brass fittings?

A decorative (yet functional) string of scoring beads ($30)? To protect your invest-ment—and don't think that a $2,000-$25,000 home pool table isn't an invest-ment—a heavier Naugahyde or vinyl table cover may be more suitable ($100–$200), or perhaps a custom leather table cover ($900).

Naturally, two or three 100-watt light bulbs are scarcely going to provide even lighting over the playing surface. The standard pool table fixtures contain three or four fluorescent lights, housed in a variety of coverings. The imitation leaded glass look is popular ($150–$300), but that only scratches the surface of the looks available in pool table lighting today. Home table owners, as well as billiard room proprietors, are beginning to realize that the light fixtures are an integral part of the overall room design. To that end, lighting companies have developed gorgeous fixtures to hover over pool tables. Leaded glass and polished brass ($1,500) can add elegance to the home billiard setting.

The number of bulbs or length of fluorescent lights varies depending on the length of the table. When choosing a multiple-globe light configuration, consider a fixture with four lamps. Three globes attempting to cover the playing area of a nine-foot table is not likely to spread ample light. Also, the fixture should be five-and-a-half to six feet in length. Three-globe configurations are adequate for eight-foot or seven-foot tables. (While extravagant fixtures with leaded glass shades and fluted oak or solid brass fixtures are beautiful pieces and more than adequate for home billiard rooms, professional players prefer the more standard long, fluorescent tube lights for competition. The fluorescent tubes tend to deliver a more even distribution of light.)

As to height, most lighting fixtures hang approximately three feet over the table. To determine the light's height, raise the fixture slowly until you notice that the illumination reaches the cushions. Don't try to light up the entire room with the table light. The general rule of thumb in lighting is that light should be evenly distributed to all areas of

(courtesy of Christies)

Looking for something really special in a home billiard table? This eighteenth century George II mahogany table can be yours for a paltry $121,000, and it even comes with cues!

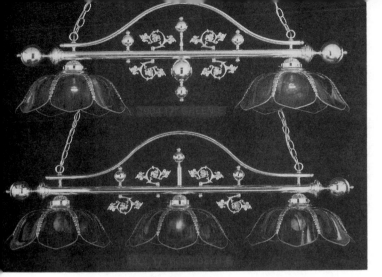

(courtesy of *Billiards Digest*)

(courtesy of *Billiards Digest*)

the table—no darker in the corners than in the center of the table.

And when setting up your home billiard room, don't forget to take care of your opponents (er, *guests*). While you're nonchalantly executing your 200-ball run in Straight Pool or cruising through your fifth consecutive rack of Nine-Ball, your guests will need a place to sit. Might I suggest a nice 34-inch-high oak spectator chair ($200–$500)? This will afford your guest some comfort during his/her inactivity—and the higher seat will assure him/her a bird's-eye view of your flawless play. Ever the perfect host!

For the final touch, posters, prints, and paintings of various pool settings are readily available through billiard dealers and/or billiard mail order companies.

Depending on space and budgetary considerations, a room in your house can be completely outfitted for as little as $2,000. Then again, a higher quality table and accessories, as mentioned above, can bring the price up rapidly to, say, $6,000. Whichever route you choose, your pool room will quickly become the most enjoyable, popular room in the house.

SELECTING EQUIPMENT

It may come as a surprise to some newcomers to pocket billiards, but the billiard industry has hundreds of product manufacturers. In recent years, nearly 100,000 pool and billiard tables have rolled out of American factories annually. Probably 10 times that many cues have been produced, along with balls, cue racks, and other accessories pertinent to the sport.

With pool enjoying a tremendous resurgence, finding a reputable billiard dealer in your area shouldn't present much of a problem. And while there are many more small, regional (sometimes local) table and cue manufacturers than I can mention, here is a list of some of the industry's heavyweights. Your local billiard supply dealer is certain to carry products from these companies.

Tables: Pool tables are like automobiles. The price range really runs the gamut, from veritable Yugos to full-fledged Rolls Royces. But, like cars, in most cases you get what you pay for.

For starters, don't settle for a table that has a wood playing bed: insist on slate. Hardwood frames are also desirable. Don't expect pressed board to last very long. The low end for slate-bed, hardwood pool tables is around $1,500. Considering the expected life of the table (it will outlast most owners . . . and that Yugo!), pool tables are still a bargain.

Between $2,500 and $5,000, you've moved into the mid-sized luxury models—the Buick Riviera and Continental Town Car range. These tables feature various expensive hardwoods, like walnut. Tables in this range

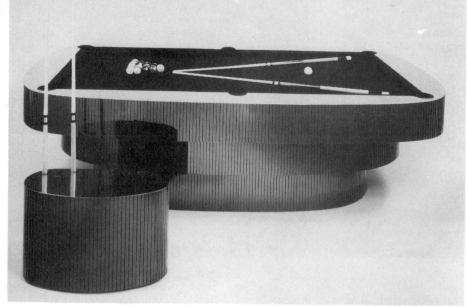

(courtesy of *Billiards Digest*)

(courtesy of *Billiards Digest*)

also feature a glossy, hand-rubbed furniture finish (as opposed to laminates) and leather pockets. The selection is also much wider, with options on leg design and finish.

If you're willing to part with more than $5,000 for your pool table, you can expect custom leather pockets, hand-turned legs, hardwood framing, custom trim, and the eternal gratitude of the billiard dealer who sells you the table. Table prices can soar into the $20,000-$30,000 range, depending on the whims of the buyer. The craftsmen in the billiard industry can do amazing things with wood (or other materials), and they love a challenge!

Among the industry leaders in pool tables are:

A. E. Schmidt Company, St. Louis, Missouri

Brunswick Billiards, Bristol, Wisconsin

Dynamo-McIntire Pool Tables, Fort Worth, Texas

Today's billiard table manufacturers are true craftsmen. Some of the higher-end pool tables available are one-of-a-kind hand-carved designs and antique replicas.
(photos courtesy of *Billiards Digest*)

Gandy's Industries, Macon, Georgia

Golden West Billiard Mfg., Canoga Park, California

Kasson Pool Table Mfg., Babbit, Minnesota

Murrey & Sons, Los Angeles, California

National Billiards, Cincinnati, Ohio

Olhausen Billiard Table Mfg., San Diego, California

Peter Vitalie Co., Rosman, North Carolina

Play Master-Renaissance, Bland, Missouri

Sterling Billiards, Rosman, North Carolina

World of Leisure, Covina, California

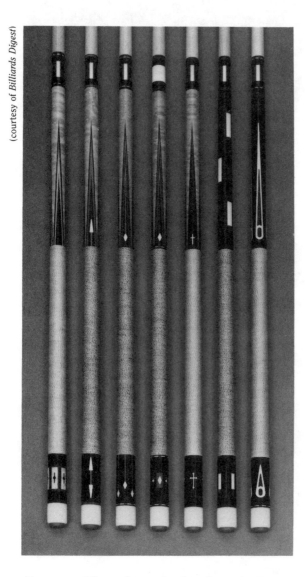

Cues: If you haven't already picked up a two-piece cue for yourself, it won't be long before you just can't live without one. However, there is no need to plunge right into a $1,000 cue stick. Some midrange production cues play as well as any custom job, and they're great to start out with. Playing with a decent production cue will give you time to determine what you like and don't like in a cue. It's very difficult to simply stroll into a billiard supply store and figure out what kind of cue you like. You have to play with the cue for a period of time. Then you'll discover whether the weight is good, the taper is long enough, the tip is small enough, or the grip is right.

Now you can go order that $1,000 Richard Black cue!

Like I said earlier, though, there is nothing wrong with a good production cue. You just aren't afforded as many options. It's like buying suits off the rack. You can still find a nice, reasonably priced suit, but you have to take it as is. The same thing holds true with production cues.

Generally, decent production cue sticks range in price from $60 to as much as $500 (the more expensive production cues have a lot of ornamentation).

Top names in production cues include:

Adam Cues, Lynbrook, New York

Black Boar Cues, Baltimore, Maryland

Dufferin, Inc., Gurnee, Illinois

Henry Mali Co., New York, New York

Heubler's Industries, Linn, Missouri

Lishan Cues, Englewood, Florida

McDermott Cue Mfg., Menomonee Falls, Wisconsin

Meucci Originals, Olive Branch, Mississippi

Palmer Billiards, Elizabeth, New Jersey

Schmelke Mfg., Rice Lake, Wisconsin

Steve Mizerak Cues, available at all K mart stores!

Viking Cue Co., Mfg., Madison, Wisconsin

Custom cues present an entirely different picture. Most of today's true custom cue makers still hand fit each and every cue they produce. These are craftsmen who make only a couple hundred cues a year. Their waiting lists are interminably long, but when the wait is finally over, you'll be glad you were patient. These cues are truly pieces of art.

One of the greatest cue makers ever to

work a lathe, Gus Szamboti, recently passed away. His legacy is evident in the way players fortunate enough to own a Szamboti treat their wands . . . and in the prices others have offered to call a Szamboti cue their own.

My choice for the new number one craftsman is my good friend Richard Black of Houston. I've used a Richard Black cue for many years. He's as dedicated and meticulous as an artist could be, and his cues are virtually extensions of your arm.

There are a handful of cue craftsmen out there, and it seems like more and more people are trying to make their names as custom cue makers. Here are a few of the top makers of custom cues:

Bert Schrager, North Hollywood, California

David Kersenbrock, Los Angeles, California

Paul Heubler, Linn, Missouri

Helmstetter Cues, Lynbrook, New York

JP Custom Cues, Green Bay, Wisconsin

Joss Cues, Baltimore, Maryland

Joss West, Colorado Springs, Colorado

Schon Cues, Milwaukee, Wisconsin

Southwest Cues, Las Vegas, Nevada

Tim Scruggs, Baltimore, Maryland

Accessories: Custom leather pockets, spectator chairs, wall racks, table covers, cue cases, lighting fixtures . . . the list of accessories available for your home billiard room is endless. You can spend as much as $600 for an oak wall rack and at least that much for a custom leather table cover. Lights run from $100 to well over $1,000.

In any case, there are a myriad of items to choose from, and here are a few of the manufacturers of products you might need:

Pockets: Cin Caro, Boulder, Colorado; Hood Leather Goods, Milwaukee, Wisconsin; Professional Leather Products, San Diego, California; R.C. Designs, Anaheim, California.

Chairs: Arkay Industries, Huntsville, Alabama; Inca Products, Chino, California; Mikhail Darafeev Co., Baldwin Park, California; Prime Wood Products, Holland, Michigan; Renaissance Wood Products, Louisville, Kentucky.

Cue Racks: Allwood Sports Products, Littleton, Colorado; Almel Industries, Tupelo, Mississippi; American Family Products, Addison, Illinois; Golden West Billiard Mfg., Canoga Park, California; Van Patten Cue Racks, Santa Fe Springs, California.

Table Covers: Professional Leather Products, San Diego, California; R.C. Designs, Anaheim, California.

Cue Cases: American Vinyl Products, Vernon, California; Centennial Cases, Houston, Texas; Creative Inventions, Canoga Park, California; Heubler's Industries, Linn, Missouri; It's George, Shreveport, Louisiana; New Image Pool, Phoenix, Arizona.

Custom-made cues, like my limited edition "Victoria," designed for me by Richard Black of Houston, may cost more than standard cues, but each one is truly a work of art.
(courtesy of Carmine R. Manicone Photography)

Lighting Fixtures: Almel Industries, Tupelo, Mississippi; American Family Products, Addison, Illinois; C. W. Choice, Los Angeles, California; Stylite Industries, Denver, Colorado; Toltec Company, Burnsville, Mississippi.

Posters, Books, Tapes, etc.: The Billiard Library, Long Beach, California.

CARE AND MAINTENANCE OF EQUIPMENT

CUE MAINTENANCE

It's not inconceivable that you'll eventually buy a cue stick that costs several hundred dollars. That's a pretty substantial investment. Like all investments, you'll want to take measures to protect it and retain its value.

The easiest way to protect your cue is to keep it in a sturdy cue case. Assuming you buy a two-piece cue, take it apart as soon as you finish playing and store it in your cue case. Whether you have a two-piece cue or several one-piece cues, remember, the cue stick is wood—and wood warps. Careless handling of your cues is the fastest way to

(courtesy of *Billiards Digest*)

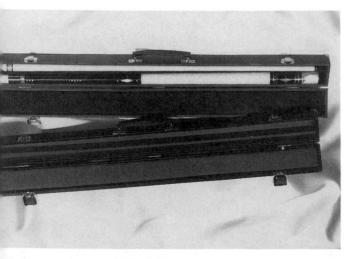

(courtesy of *Billiards Digest*)

ruin them. Don't ever leave your cue leaning against a wall for extended periods. Keep your cues in a case or in a cue rack. Also, don't store cues in places that are subject to temperature extremes—like the trunk of your car, your garage, or near a window.

Aside from those fairly basic rules, your cue requires very little maintenance. Only two areas of your cue need more than passing attention: the shaft and the tip. The shaft of the cue tends to acquire a sticky buildup over time. It can even get a tad on the unsightly side. To remedy the situation, you can wipe the cue down with a damp cloth. Just remember to dry the stick off immediately. Another way to return the shaft to a slick, smooth surface is to fold a hundred-dollar bill in half, wrap it around the shaft, and slide the bill up and down. The bill will clean off some

(courtesy of Carmine R. Manicone Photography)

When taking a cue from the cue rack (or returning it to the rack), watch what you're doing. Don't yank the stick out with one hand, especially if the tip is covered. You're sure to damage the tip and ferrule, and you'll put undue stress on the shaft.

The part of your cue that will require the most attention is the tip. A seemingly harmless little chunk of leather, the tip may just be the most important element (functionally) of that $250 cue you just bought. All of the glitzy ornamentation in the world won't save your game if you try to play it with an inferior cue tip. The cue ball responds to the tip, and nothing else.

How important is the tip? Anytime you hit the cue ball off center, the tip must grab that cue ball and impart on it the spin you desire. A bad tip—one that is flat, too round, too worn, or too smooth—will cause a miscue. (A miscue occurs when there is no

(courtesy of Carmine R. Manicone Photography)

Use two hands and gently pull the butt end of the cue out first. That will make it easier to glide the cue out of the rack safely.

of the grime and tends to give the shaft a slick, polished feel. (Okay—in reality, the denomination of the bill makes no difference. But, psychologically, bigger bills do seem to add greater luster to the shaft!) If the shaft is particularly sticky or dirty, a last resort—but be *very careful* here—is to gently stroke the shaft with a *very fine* grade sandpaper (400 or 600). *Never* allow the paper to touch the ivory ferrule that separates the wood shaft from the cue tip. It scratches very easily. And don't stroke so hard that you reduce the diameter of the shaft. You'll wind up with a pencil in your hands!

friction between the tip and cue ball. The tip simply slides off the cue ball.)

A good leather cue tip should be somewhat rough. The roughness allows the tip to hold chalk, which in turn is what causes friction with the cue ball. In essence, the tip grabs the cue ball for an instant, allowing the desired spin to be transferred to the cue ball.

Once, I went down to the Bahamas. No one knew who I was. I went to this poolroom to play and pulled a cue out of the rack that was severely warped. I chose that cue because it was the only cue that had a decent tip. I could adjust for the fact that the stick was warped, but I would not have been able to do anything to compensate for a lousy tip. You can't make up for not being able to do anything with the cue ball. I used that warped cue stick and played very well.

It's important to realize that the tip on your new cue probably has not been shaped properly. It will be free of chalk and will look a bit flat. That's normal. But don't chalk up just yet! You have to shape your tip.

What you are searching for when shaping your tip is a curve similar to that of a

(courtesy of Carmine R. Manicone Photography)

Don't be intimidated by a tip scuffer. Use it to rough up the leather on your cue tip so that it will hold chalk.

nickel. To achieve this, file down the edge of the tip with 200- or 400-grade sandpaper. As always, be careful not to allow the sandpaper (or file) to touch the ivory ferrule. The edge of the tip should not hang over at all. By the same token, don't make the tip too round—like the head of a bullet. A tip that's too round will glance right off the cue ball.

Once you've shaped your new tip, scuff up the top of the tip with a coarser sandpaper (60-grade) or a rasp (a piece of metal with indentations). Again, this is to create tiny pores so the tip will hold chalk. Most billiard supply stores stock what we call "tip tappers" or "scuffers." They're small metal rasps made especially for cue tips. Here's a little secret, though. I recently got caught on the road without my tip tapper. I went to a local drug store and picked up a Dr. Scholl's "Callous Remover." It's a sandpaper-like surface with a handle, and it worked great!

Your new tip will likely have to be reshaped after a month or so of play. The natural compression the tip endures from striking the cue ball causes it to lose its shape. If you have a good, hard tip, you should only have to reshape it that one time. After that, it should last for quite a while. If you find that your tip is losing its shape too frequently, you may have a soft tip. Most pros prefer hard tips. If you'd rather have a hard tip, take your cue to a qualified cue repairman and have him change it.

Now that you've spent all that effort shaping your tip just so, make sure you chalk it properly.

I've seen countless beginners and amateurs walk into a poolroom and grab a house cue. If it has a super-round, glass-smooth tip, they think it's great. Then they go to the table and search out the piece of chalk that has a nice, deep groove in it. It fits over the tip of the cue like a hat. Stop right there!

For starters, we already know that a tip that is too round isn't good. Also, if the tip is so smooth that it won't accept any new chalk,

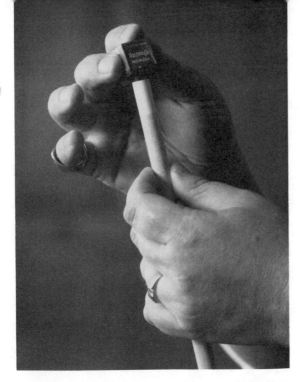

The path to a clean ferrule and a consistently chalked tip begins with proper technique. Hold the chalk in one hand, and gently turn the tip with your other hand. Remember to watch the tip to be sure the chalk is adhering evenly.
(courtesy of Carmine R. Manicone Photography)

It doesn't take a rocket scientist to figure out which cue tip has been well maintained. Notice the perfectly rounded leather tip and shiny, straight edge of the top cue. The ferrule is pearly white. The tip of the bottom cue is virtually useless. It's flat on top, and the edge has "spread" to the point that it extends beyond the width of the ferrule. Because of improper chalking, the ferrule is dirty and has a chalky ring around it. Disgusting!
(courtesy of Carmine R. Manicone Photography)

you need to scuff it up. Finally, that worn-out piece of chalk won't do anything except put an ugly, blue ring around your ferrule!

When chalking your cue, remember that you want a nice, even surface of chalk. The chalk should be granular, not cakey. Humidity tends to make chalk cakey. New chalk tends to be too hard. The best piece of chalk is usually one that's just partially used.

The proper way to chalk your cue is to gently brush it onto the tip. Don't chalk from side to side. Don't spin the tip into the chalk. With your left hand, hold the cue just beneath the ferrule. With your right hand, hold the chalk at a slight angle and brush it against the tip. And don't chalk while looking at the table or in another direction. Keep your eyes on the tip to make sure the entire tip is holding chalk.

As with the sandpaper, try not to touch your ferrule with the chalk. If you develop a ring around the ferrule, you're not chalking properly.

TABLE CARE

The main thing to remember about your home pool table is that it's not simply a piece of sports equipment—it is a piece of furniture.

For starters, make sure your home table is installed by a trained billiard table professional. It's worth a few dollars to be sure the slate bed is installed properly and is level. The cushions need to be set at the right height and angle, and the cloth should be snug.

Once installed, a pool table requires minimal care. In fact, keeping the playing surface clean is about all that's left for you to do. Even if you have a leather or vinyl table cover, the cloth will get dirty over time. Dust, talcum powder, and chalk settle in the cloth.

Hand-held vacuum cleaners offer the quickest remedy. Just be sure that the agitating brush on the cleaner head is not overly

(courtesy of *Billiards Digest*)

The only part of your home pool table that needs frequent attention is the cloth. When brushing, move in one direction, from the head of the table to the foot.

(courtesy of *Billiards Digest*)

A slightly damp cloth is all that's needed to keep the rails clean and shiny.

abrasive. Pool-table cloth is a pretty finely woven wool/nylon blend. Don't abuse it. (Avoid using industrial-strength vacuum cleaners!)

If you'd rather play it safe, a soft-bristled hand brush is the conventional way to clean a pool table. Most new tables are equipped with such a brush. Always brush in one direction—from the head of the table toward the rack. And don't forget to brush the cushions.

The rails, whether wood or laminate, can be wiped down occasionally with a damp cloth.

Probably the easiest way to maintain a quality playing surface is to keep your pool table just that—a pool table. Don't let your table become a work bench or utility table on which you fold all your laundry. Keep children from using the bed of the table as a battlefield and using the space beneath the table for a fort.

Properly maintained, your home pool table should last forever.

Glossary

Angle: The intersecting of two lines, which determines the desired path of either the cue ball or the object ball; *i.e.*, the point at which the cue ball must contact an object ball in order to send that object ball to a pocket.

Balance Point: The point on a cue stick at which the stick's weight is evenly distributed. Normally 16-20 inches up from the butt end of the cue.

Bank Shot: A shot in which the object ball is driven into one or more cushions on its path to a pocket. (This does not include a ball's incidental contact with a rail, as sometimes happens when an object ball is shot along a rail.)

Bed (or **Table Bed**): The playing area on a pocket billiard table.

Billiard: In pocket billiard games, when the cue ball purposely glances off one object ball and into another object ball. (Not to be confused with a combination shot, in which the cue ball strikes an object ball, sending that object ball into one or more additional object balls.)

Bottle (or **Shake Bottle**): A plastic or leather container used to hold numbered "peas" or pills." The bottle and pills are used in various pocket billiard games, like Kelly Pool and Pea Pool.

Break (or **Opening Break**): The opening shot of all pocket billiard games, requirements of which are spelled out in the rules of the various pocket games. In Snooker, the total points scored in one inning of play.

Break Shot: In 14.1 Continuous pocket billiards (Straight Pool), the first shot following the pocketing of the fourteenth ball of a rack. (After the fourteenth ball is pocketed, the fifteenth ball remains in position while the 14 pocketed balls are re-racked. The break shot is critical in continuing a player's turn at the table.)

Bridge: The configuration of the front hand, which holds and guides the shaft end of the cue stick (see also **Mechanical Bridge**).

Butt: The larger end of a cue stick. On a two-piece cue, the half of the stick that contains the grip.

Called Ball: When playing Call Shot, the object ball designated by the shooter to be pocketed.

Called Pocket: When playing Call Shot, the pocket into which the called object ball is intended to be made.

Call Shot: A stipulation in pocket billiard games that requires the shooter to announce (or call), prior to shooting, the object ball he intends to pocket, as well as the pocket into which the ball will be made.

Carom: In pocket billiards, the result of a ball glancing off another ball or rail.

Center Spot: The center point on a pocket billiard or carom billiard table. The center point is used as a position for spotted balls in the rules of some billiard games.

Chalk: A dry carbonate of lime which adheres to the cue tip and keeps the tip from sliding off the cue ball in an undesired manner upon contact.

Combination: The pocketing of an object ball through contact with another object ball.

Corner Hooked: A situation in which the tip of a pocket disturbs the direct path from the cue ball to an object ball.

Count: A successful shot or score. A term primarily used in Rotation, in which a player earns points commensurate with the number on the object ball pocketed.

Cripple: A virtually unmissable shot.

Cross-Corner: A shot that sends a ball off a side rail and to the opposite corner pocket.

Cross-Side: A shot in which a ball is banked off a side rail into the opposite side pocket.

Crutch: Another term for the mechanical bridge.

Cue: A tapered stick used to strike the cue ball in pocket billiards.

Cue Ball: The white ball used in pocket billiard games. It is always the ball initially struck by the cue on pocket billiard shots.

Cue-Ball-in-Hand: A rule that allows the cue ball to be placed anywhere on the table bed prior to the next shot.

Cue-Ball-in-Hand Behind Head String: A rule which allows the cue ball to be placed anywhere between the head string and the top rail, so long as it is not touching an object ball.

Cue Tip: The rounded leather tip attached to the end of the cue which makes initial contact with the cue ball.

Cushion: The rubber, cloth-covered rail fastened along the inner border of a billiard table.

Cut Shot: Any shot in which the cue ball does not strike the object ball flush, also called an angled shot.

Dead Shot: A configuration of two or more object balls, all touching, whereby at least one object ball has a natural path to a specific pocket. (The surrounding balls will not allow the object ball to move in any direction other than toward a specific pocket.)

Diamonds: The decorative markings along the rails of a pocket billiard table. Used by some players as reference points for determining aim on carom or bank shots.

Double Hit: An illegal shot in which the cue ball is struck twice by the cue tip on a single stroke.

Draw: Applying reverse spin to the cue ball by stroking well below the ball's center resulting in the cue ball rolling backward after contact with the object ball.

Drop Pockets: A pocket billiard table on which there is no ball-return gulley. Pocketed balls remain in the pocket in which they were made.

English: The general term to describe the spin applied to the cue ball by striking the ball off center.

Feather Shot: A shot in which the cue ball barely touches the object ball. An exaggerated version of the cut shot.

Ferrule: The protective sleeve at the top end of a cue stick, upon which the cue tip is affixed.

Follow: The opposite of draw. Applying a forward spin to the cue ball by stroking well above the ball's center, the result being that the cue ball continues to roll forward after contact with the object ball.

Follow-through: The continuation of the stroke after contact with the cue ball has been completed.

Foot of the Table: The end of the pocket

billiard table at which the balls are racked.

Foot Spot: The spot on which the apex ball rests when racking balls in pocket billiard games. Point where imaginary lines running from the second diamonds along the side rails and middle diamonds along the end rails intersect.

Foot String: The line running from the second diamond along one side rail, through the foot spot, to the second diamond along the opposite side rail.

Force Draw and **Force Follow:** A stroke which produces extreme draw or extreme follow.

Foul: An infraction of the rules of a pocket billiard game, resulting in a penalty as determined by the rules of that particular game.

Frame: One full turn at the table by each opponent. Inning.

Frozen: The term that describes a ball resting in contact with a cushion or another ball.

Full Ball: Contact on direct line between a cue ball and object ball. Not struck at an angle.

Game Ball: The ball which effectively ends a game.

Grip: The placement of the back hand on the butt end of the cue.

Gulley Table: A pocket billiard table which features channels that return pocketed balls to a ball box at the foot end of the table.

Handicap: Scoring and rules modifications to accommodate players of varying skill levels.

Head of Table: The end of a pocket billiard table from which the break shot is taken.

Head Spot: A point intersected by an imaginary line from the middle diamonds along the end rails and the second diamonds along the side rails at the head of the table.

Head String: Line at the head of the table running from the second diamond along the side rail, through the head spot, to the second diamond along the opposite side rail.

High Run: In 14.1 Continuous (otherwise known as Straight Pool), the most consecutive balls pocketed in a single turn at the table (inning).

Inning: A player's completed turn at the table.

Jaw: The angled portions of the cushion at the mouth of a pocket.

Jawed Ball: A ball that rattles between the jaws of a pocket, preventing the ball from dropping into the pocket.

Joint: The part of a two-piece cue at which the shaft and butt ends are joined.

Jumped Ball: A ball that has left the playing bed, resulting in a foul and loss of turn.

Jump Shot: A shot in which the cue ball (or on some occasions an object ball) is propelled over an obstructing ball.

Key Ball: In 14.1 Continuous, the fourteenth ball in a rack. The ball which precedes the break shot.

Kick Shot: A shot in which the cue ball caroms off one or more cushions before making contact with an object ball.

Kiss Shot: An occurrence in which the cue ball or an object ball makes contact more than once. Also similar to a carom shot, in which the cue ball or an object ball contacts a second object ball for the purpose of completing a shot. In some cases, a kiss may impede the intended path of the cue ball or object ball; *i.e.*, the first object ball contacted may carom back into the path of the cue ball, kissing the cue ball and disrupting it from its natural path.

Kitchen: The playing area between the head string and the cushion at the head of the table.

Lagging for Break: To determine which player has the option of breaking to begin a pocket billiard game, players generally lag—each shooting a ball from behind the head string to the foot rail and back toward the head rail. The player whose ball stops closest to the head rail is given the break option.

Leave: The term used to describe the table layout after a player has completed a shot.

Long: Widening the natural angle of the cue ball's path off a cushion or object ball through the use of English, or spin.

Masse: A shot in which extreme English is applied to the cue ball by elevating the cue stick to a severe angle, between 45 and 90 degrees, and striking down at the cue ball.

Mechanical Bridge: A grooved plate affixed to the tip of a stick which provides a guide for the cue stick on shots for which a normal bridge cannot easily be made.

Miscue: Imperfect contact between the cue tip and cue ball, normally the result of excessive English, inadequate application of chalk, or a defective tip.

Miss: Simply, the failure to legally pocket a ball.

Natural: Normally associated with carom billiards, a shot whereby no compensatory English or angle is needed for successful execution.

Object Ball: In pocket billiards, any ball other than the cue ball.

Opening Break: See **Break**.

Open Table: In Eight-Ball, when the choice of group (solid colored balls or striped balls) has not yet been decided, the table is deemed to be open.

Peas: Small numbered balls that fit into the Bottle or Shake Bottle, used in various pocket billiard games.

Pills: See **Peas**.

Playing Position: A predetermined plan of action by which a player attempts to legally pocket an object ball and direct the cue ball to a spot from which he can pocket another object ball.

Pool: The common term for pocket billiards.

Powder: Talc applied to the bridge hand to assure smooth, easy movement of the cue stick's shaft through the bridge.

Push Shot: A stroke on which the cue tip maintains its contact with the cue ball longer than considered normal, or shoving the cue ball forward without using a back swing. Considered an illegal stroke.

Pyramid: A seldom-used term to describe the placement of the object balls in a triangular configuration at the start of most pocket billiard games.

Race: The number of games required to win a set or match in tournament play; *i.e.*, a race to nine, meaning the first player to reach nine games wins the set or match.

Rack: The wooden or plastic frame used to group the object balls at the beginning of pocket billiard games. Various shaped racks are available, depending on the game. Eight-Ball, Nine-Ball, and Seven-Ball utilize different racks. Also used to describe the general grouping of balls prior to the start of a pocket billiard game.

Rails: The top ledges of a pocket billiard table not covered by cloth, from which the cushions extend.

Reverse English: Spin applied to the cue ball contrary to the ball's natural direction.

Round Robin: A tournament format in which each player plays each contestant at least once.

Run: Consecutive balls, games, or points successfully tallied by a player; *i.e.*, a player may run 150 consecutive balls in Straight Pool, 12 consecutive points in Three-Cushion billiards, or five consecutive racks of Nine-Ball.

Running English: The spin applied to the cue ball, causing the ball to carom off a cushion at a wide angle.

Safety: A defensive maneuver intended to keep the opponent from scoring.

Scratch: A foul, which usually occurs when the cue ball is pocketed.

Shaft: The narrower, tapered end of a cue stick, on which the tip is affixed.

Shake Bottle: See **Bottle**.

Single Elimination: A tournament format in which a single loss constitutes elimination from competition.

Slate: A quarried and finished bed of stone which serves as the playing bed on quality pool tables.

Snookered: The inability, due to an obstructing object ball or pocket jaw, to shoot the cue ball on a direct path to the intended object ball.

Spot: The decal used to mark the foot spot, center spot, or head spot on a billiard table.

Spot Shot: A shot when the cue ball is on the head spot and an object ball is on the foot spot.

Spotting a Ball: The replacement of balls as determined by the rules of the game being played.

Stop Shot: Striking the cue ball in such a way that it stops upon contact with the object ball.

Stroke: The completed movement of the cue stick in striking the cue ball.

Thin Hit: A shot in which the cue ball barely grazes the object ball.

Throw Shot: Altering the path of one or more object balls through the application of spin on the cue ball.

Triangle: The rack used to position the object balls in most pocket billiard games. Can accommodate all 15 object balls.

Index